CRITICS' COMMENTS

Travis offers passionate insight into corporate racism

"His message is straightforward and perhaps shocking to those in the corporate world who believe that both law and cultural change have diminished racism in U.S. businesses and opened up many opportunities for Blacks seeking to join, and progress in, the ranks of management."

William Neikirk
Chicago Tribune

Black execs find there's room at the top for discrimination

"In this book, Chicago author Dempsey J. Travis captures the personal struggle of African-American executives and other professionals to overcome racism and achieve their full potential. It is based on 122 interviews with black men and women who have endured racism in Fortune 500 corporations, prestigious universities, leading hospitals, the military, the media, the banking industry, employment agencies, religion and country clubs ... The anguish, rage, fear, shock and despair described by these veterans in the battle against racism grabs the reader on an emotional level and does not let go."

Timothy Crawford
Chicago Sun-Times

"*Racism: American Style, A Corporate Gift* is compelling in its startling revelation."

Earl Calloway
Chicago Defender

OTHER BOOKS BY DEMPSEY J. TRAVIS

Harold: The People's Mayor

Real Estate is the Gold in Your Future

An Autobiography of Black Politics

An Autobiography of Black Jazz

An Autobiography of Black Chicago

Don't Stop Me Now

RACISM:
AMERICAN STYLE

A CORPORATE GIFT

DEMPSEY J. TRAVIS

Library of Congress Cataloging-in-Publication Data

Travis, Dempsey, 1920–
    Racism-American style : corporate gift / by Dempsey J. Travis.—1st ed.
        p.   cm.
    Includes bibliographical references and index.
    ISBN 0-941484-09-2 : $17.95
    1. Discrimination in employment—United States. 2. Afro-American
executives—United States. I. Title.
HD4903.5.U58T75   1991
331.6'996073—dc20   90–12434
                                                                        CIP

First Printing, June 1990
Second Printing, October 1990

DEDICATION

This work is dedicated to the
multitude of African-Americans who
entrusted me with their stories.

ACKNOWLEDGMENTS

Over five decades, Duke Ellington and his orchestra garnered international acclaim. Year after year they turned out hit after hit. "East St. Louis Toodle-Oo," 1927; "The Mooche," 1928; "Mood Indigo," 1931; "Sophisticated Lady," 1933; and "Solitude," 1934, were among their earliest successes.

Ellington was noted particularly for attracting and retaining such great musicians as Johnny Hodges, alto sax; Cootie Williams, trumpet; Lawrence Brown, trombone; Harry Carney, baritone sax; Sonny Greer, drums; and composer Billy Strayhorn.

My success as a writer cannot approach that of Ellington, the musician. However, for the decade that I have directed a literary orchestra, we have produced five successive hits: *An Autobiography of Black Chicago*, 1981; *An Autobiography of Black Jazz*, 1983; *An Autobiography of Black Politics*, 1987; *Real Estate is the Gold in Your Future*, 1988; and *Harold: The People's Mayor*, 1989.

The credit for these best-sellers is shared with my literary ensemble: Ruby Davis, senior researcher; Catherine Jones, administrative assistant; Dorothy Parr Riesen, editor; Orville A. Hurt, artist; and my wife Moselynne, who has adjusted to the peculiar sleeping habits of a writer.

FOREWORD

I have known Dempsey Travis for many years. Not only is he a successful real estate man, but he is an African-American real estate man who has wrestled his entire life against the disease of racism. Therefore, when he writes about *Racism: American Style A Corporate Gift,* he sensitively deals with the effects of corporate racism from personal experience. As he relates the stories of thwarted lives cut down by personal and institutional racism, one feels the rage of talented people forced to wear protective masks. While it is impossible as a European American to experience what it means to be Black in America, this book gives one a glimpse into the daily frustration and rage that is the lot of African Americans.

Ever since the civil rights revolution of the 1960s, many whites in this country have concluded that a large percentage of Black people have made it into the secure areas of middle management and in the professions. The assumption has been that once out of the economic ghetto, the struggle against racism has been won. This book makes it abundantly clear that in America the struggle against racist stereotypes and accompanying rejection is never over. As some people have said, African Americans are never more than one pay check away from the ghetto.

In this book, Dempsey Travis has reminded all Americans, Black and white, that as we face the 21st century we are confronted with a persistent and growing racism that is threatening our very existence as a nation. Deep personal prejudice embedded in the psyche of white Americans seems tolerable when held in control. But when this prejudice is coupled with decision-making power and becomes systematically institutionalized in the economic, political and social fabric of a nation, it assumes a frightening dimension. It is not enough for whites to be concerned with their personal attitudes, important as they are. We must also commit ourselves to anti-racist activity. This means confronting the institutional arrangements of our society with a full understanding that they work as a barrier for people of color.

The issue of racism has again become a high priority on the American agenda whether we like it or not. This time around it may be even more difficult because its practice has become more sophisticated. It is masked now in terms of efficiency and productivity. Then, too, the churches, which have operated as the conscience of America, have withdrawn into what appears to be a navel-gazing spirituality. Because it is essentially a white problem, people of color may have little interest or patience in helping whites to grapple with the issue.

Yet, there is no alternative. We have said for a long time that no nation can exist half slave and half free. Communication among us is necessary but it's not enough. A joint commitment to racial and economic justice is the only avenue left.

Thank you Dempsey Travis for revealing to us again the tragedy and persistence of white racism.

Rev. Don Benedict
Executive Director, Clergy and Laity Concerned

INTRODUCTION

We have all had experiences so searing that we keep them secrets from our families and best friends. The events are usually demeaning and degrading.

I once saw a proud Black man with whom I was slightly acquainted kicked in his buttocks by a young white manager of a chain shoe store because he had forgotten to perform some task. I left the store immediately because I wanted to spare this man the embarrassment of knowing that I had seen him Tom. He Tommed, and the manager was saved from the expense of buying himself a new set of front teeth.

Twenty-five years have passed since that humiliation occurred, but I feel safe in saying the former assistant shoe store manager never shared that incident with his wife or his father, who was a prominent physician in Chicago. Currently, I have some social contact with this elite-acting, peacock-walking, nose-in-the-air individual who does not have the slightest notion that we share a secret, one that I have never revealed.

This book is about the thousands of African-Americans who are figuratively kicked in their posteriors by the straw bosses of corporate America daily as they attempt to scale the ladders of opportunity. Many of my interviewees have buried the pain of racism so deep inside of their subconscious that the only voice that emerges through their lips is that of Blacks talking white.

Some Blacks who are vicariously white are included in this work to bring a balanced perspective to the Black experience.

But it is the experiences of Black legends who through the centuries have thundered their messages without fear that we honor most. The men and women who speak through these pages relate the realities that Black Americans have faced in the 20th century. They tell true stories that should engage and enlighten readers from every ethnic background.

The refusal to open one's mind to the painful truths of our society is to choose the darkness of the cave rather than the brightness of the sunlight.

Dempsey J. Travis
July 1990

CONTENTS

BLACKS: THE CORPORATE OUTSIDERS

In the blossoming months of the first year in the last decade of the 20th century, blacks are still corporate outsiders in that they have not been permitted to become members of corporate America's favorite "deal making" playground, the country club. In interviewing 122 Black executives, both male and female, employed by corporate America, I did not find a single corporate Black at any level who held an individual membership in an establishment country club or who could lay claim to even having a loose connection to the good old boys network.

However, it is a tradition for the historically "white only" Commonwealth Club in Richmond, Va., to extend the governor a personal invitation to become a member of the hallowed temple of Virginia's political elite. Douglas L. Wilder, America's first elected Black governor since Reconstruction, graciously declined the bid with the explanation that "he belonged to enough clubs right now." Almost a decade earlier when he was the lone Black state senator, he had been deserted by his powerful Democratic colleagues, who refused to accompany him into the Commonwealth Club for lunch.

On the other hand, I have a personal friend who is a Black multimillionaire businessman who owns a $750,000 home located within five feet of the 16th hole of the Olympia Fields Country Club.

He cannot join because he was blackballed by the members of that organization. He was once extended an invitation to become a member of the club by two white liberals. However, that invitation was quickly withdrawn when the two potential sponsors were threatened with expulsion from the club. As we approached the 21st Century, Blacks and women are still excluded from the Bob O'Link, Butler National, Old Elm and thousands of other country clubs. According to Mike Royko, nationally syndicated columnist for the *Chicago Tribune*, an exception was made when, in early 1990, Michael Jordan, one of America's most admired athletes, and one of the highest-paid basketball players in the annals of the game, was accepted in the Wynstone Country Club in North Barrington, Ill.

Olympia Fields Country Club members may invite an individual guest no more than seven times per season. My friend is invited from time to time to play golf as a guest of a WASP neighbor. Unlike his white neighbor, he is in the awkward position of not being able to invite a house guest to play a game of golf on a course that is literally in his back yard. The Black achiever cannot explain this exclusionary phenomenon to his children, who sit in their window and watch white kids their age playing golf daily, except in the context of being Black and being a victim of white racism.

It is an on-going responsibility of African-American parents to teach their children that they are living in a society that has refused to extend to people of color full membership in Club America after keeping them on the waiting list for 400 years. The mother and father of Mary Jo Baker recognized their responsibility and the need to prepare their daughter to be forever vigilant in a milieu that is infested with corporate barracudas.

Hence, when Mary Jo was recruited on the Spelman College campus in Atlanta, Ga., for a job with a Fortune 500 company in New York City, her father went out and bought her an ugly "Made in America" inflatable copper-colored doll with exaggerated Negroid features. Mr. Baker, like the doll's manufacturer, did not want Mary Jo to forget where and who she was. To further drive his point home, Mr. Baker instructed Mary Jo to take the ugly babydoll to New York City with her and keep it in the middle of her bed as a constant reminder of her Black Georgian roots each night when she returned home from the office.

As an outsider, one must hold on to one's roots in order to stay on the sanity track. Mary Jo's initial validation as an official outsider became evident to her when she was invited to a cocktail party for junior executives given by her employer. The first thing she noticed when she walked into the gala affair at the New York Hilton was that the few visible Blacks (there are some Blacks who look and pass for white) who were present had gravitated to the corner of the room like a huddling football squad.

Mary Jo decided she would be gregarious and join one of the many conversation bouquets at the party. The first group of three people that she introduced herself to took a brief glance at her and continued to talk to each other, acting as if she was the invisible spook who sat behind the door. Thus, she about faced and briskly stepped away to join another animated triangle, hoping to make it a quartet. Although she was close enough to blow in their ears, they totally ignored Mary Jo and remained a white triad. Rather than stand there continuing to look and feel like a fool, she moved on to another bouquet. By this time Mary Jo, who is a shapely 5'7" tall, attractive hazel-eyed brunette, began to feel as downhearted and low as someone who had been urinated on by a skunk. However, she refused to be daunted and thus kept moving around the room until she finally found a mix-gendered configuration of five who acknowledged her presence and treated her with the proper social graces.

The outsider treatment that Mary Jo was introduced to at her first executive cocktail party is typical of what happens repeatedly to most Blacks on such occasions. However, she was different in that she was aggressive and continued to try to socially integrate after a first, second and third rejection. Most Black men are not as naive as Mary Jo in that they would have stopped circulating after the first rebuff and joined the "B" team or simply made a quiet exit, if there were no other Blacks present. Many Blacks avoid the white corporate cocktail circuit unless it is job related and absolutely mandatory because they have found that amidst the clinking of wine glasses, the laughter, the deal making and the golf talk, is a lonely and isolated individual who nine times out of 10 is Black.

Following 13 years on the corporate cocktail circuit, Mary Jo gave the following rationale for attending such events:

> Although I am extremely uncomfortable, I feel that being
> there has some validity because at least it causes the
> establishment people to have to deal with my presence,
> whether they want to or not. Whether they talk to me or

not, they are very conscious of the fact that a Black person is in the room.

Although I am frequently distressed, I still force myself to go to those kinds of cocktail gatherings. The years have taught me that I don't have to stay for the final curtain. I simply go on and make my cameo appearance and get the heck off the stage. My life is worth something to me and I don't need to sit or stand around getting indigestion eating finger food, drinking wine and umbrelling my depressed feelings with a smile.

I don't care what people say, nobody really wants to be rejected. That's difficult. Regardless of the bravado one may bring to the setting, it still hurts.

Occasionally you will attend an event and find some thoughtful white folk with the empathy to recognize that you are uncomfortable being one of a few Blacks in an all-white gathering, much the same as most of them would be out of sorts in an all-Black situation. The sensitivity of some whites permits them to embrace strangers of color in an attempt to defrost the atmosphere, as opposed to freezing them out.

Freezing the Black boy out is a standard operations procedure in the ranks of the corporate middle management people. Once a Black man enters the cloistered world of corporate America, he better be prepared for chemical warfare because the environment is filled with toxic substances. To prepare new recruits for the corporate battlefield, a colleague of mine frequently gives mini-lectures on the need for Blacks to wear gas masks. He states the following:

The structure you are about to enter is called corporate America. Within that structure is a toxic substance. It is selective. It does not attack everybody. Blacks who inhale a large quantity of fumes in this environment suffer catastrophic results. Thus, I strongly recommend that you always wear a gas mask.

The difficulty with having Blacks accept my advice is that 90 percent of the people that you see in corporate America are white and they are not wearing gas masks. So you question the need to wear this uncomfortable, hot, encumbering object, particularly since you must put it on everytime you enter the corporate environment.

The proof that supports my contention for wearing the gas mask is the fact that everyone that I know who has taken off their mask is dead.

People who have pulled off their gas masks in the middle of the day and begin gasping and choking to death usually say with their final breath, 'Nobody else was wearing a mask in my department.'

What they really mean is that they weren't doing anything that their white counterpart was not doing.

For example, a Black person is the marketing representative for his company. In this position, he accepts gifts and entertainment favors from a corporate customer, which is against company rules. But these rules are more frequently violated than obeyed. The marketing rep was fired, but some whites who committed the same indiscretions are still with the company. The Black man didn't do anything anybody else wasn't doing. He just simply got caught off guard without his gas mask.

I know a Black female sales representative who asked a supplier for a contribution to a legitimate charity, a common practice. The supplier mentioned the contribution to somebody else in the company and an anonymous letter was sent to the representative's immediate supervisor. The big boss got into the act. He, in turn, went to the supplier and the supplier verified the contribution. The sales representative was fired. She was obviously working without a mask.

The woman was stupid. If you're Black and you know you're in a hostile environment, it's for certain that you shouldn't emulate or follow practices that are common courtesies among white folks.

The subject of the final illustration is a woman planning for a vacation. A company supplier came to her and said, 'I understand you're getting ready to go down to the Caribbean Islands. I have a villa down there. Feel free to use it. I can seldom find the time to get down to Jamaica. It just doesn't get used enough.' The lady took advantage of the offer and took a small group of friends down to enjoy the sun. There was no money exchanged. Although there was no malice aforethought, the story got back to the company and the woman was fired. She became another casualty because she took off her gas mask too soon.

Statistically, as reflected in the following table, there was only a small number of Black college graduates recruited to train for middle management jobs in corporate America during the decade of the 1960s, and the tenure was short for those who selected not to wear a gas mask.

Recruitment Visits of Corporations to Predominantly Black Colleges and Universities

	number of corporations interviewing job candidates		
	1960	*1965*	*1970*
Atlanta University	0	160	510
Howard University	–	100	619
Clark College	0	40	350
Alabama A&M College	0	0	100
Alabama State College	0	7	30
Hampton Institute	20	247	573
Jackson State College	–	–	280
Johnson C. Smith University	0	25	175
Morehouse College	–	–	300
Miles	0	12	54
Norfolk State Campus (Virginia State)	5	100	250
North Carolina A&T State Univ.	6	80	517
Prairie View A&M College	–	–	350
Southern University and A&M College	0	25	600
Southern University at New Orleans	0	5	75
Texas Southern University	0	69	175
Tuskegee Institute	50	85	404
Virginia State College, Petersburg	0	25	325
Virginia Union University	5	25	150
Winston-Salem State College	–	–	25
Xavier University	0	44	185
Average per school	4	50	297

Source: R. Freeman (1976:142)

Twenty years after this data was recorded, American business executives gazing into the 1990s, and beyond, carry the burden of their failure to include a proportionate number of qualified minorities and women in top executive ranks. Data for the 1980s, though incomplete, indicate no dramatic increase in corporate recruitment of qualified students from predominantly Black institutions of higher education.

Older Black college graduates who were already in the job market were aggressively recruited for executive training programs at the annual National Association for the Advancement of Colored People (NAACP) and the National Urban League conventions between the years of 1965 and 1970. Corporate America wanted the best and the brightest. They put the selective few through rigorous psychological and educational attainment tests to assure themselves that the applicants were more qualified than any other Black they had on board.

During an interview, Bill Tatum asked the recruiter, "How many executives are presently working for the company?"

The recruiter replied, "Four thousand."

"How many Blacks do you have?" Tatum snapped.

The recruiter answered, "We never have kept those kinds of records."

"Since this is the personnel department, how many do you know?" Bill Tatum retorted.

The recruiter scratched his head and said, "Well, I'll tell you. This program is a relatively new one with us."

With a puzzled look on his face, Tatum asked, "Well, how many do you have?"

"We have two," the recruiter responded. "However, if everything goes well and you are accepted, you would actually be the third member in this training program."

The recruiter further noted the fact that just because there were only two Blacks in the training program it was not an act of exclusion by the corporation. "The subject of recruiting Blacks just never came up," he said.

Bill Tatum passed the tests and interviews with flying colors and entered the management training program for the Kyn Corporation. He described the experience as follows:

As a part of the training program, you were to spend some time working in each department. Therefore, I was sent out to one of the branch stores. When I walked into the branch manager's office and introduced myself to his secretary, she gave me a very cold and stiff reception and directed me to have a seat. There was also a young white fellow by the name of Michael O'Donnell sitting there waiting to see the manager. It turns out that he was an off-the-street walk-in seeking employment who had left his resume with the secretary the day before. When the store manager came out of his office he said, 'Wow, this is a proud day for the store. This is the first time we've ever had a headquarter trainee at our store. I'm very proud to welcome you.'

He then walked over to the white guy and shook his hand. I said, 'Pardon me sir, I'm the trainee from headquarters.'

'You are Bill Tatum?' he asked.

'That's right,' I replied.

He looked at me for a moment frozen in time, and said, 'I welcome both of you fellows to the store.'

The manager then swiveled his head toward Michael O'Donnell and said, 'Your training starts tomorrow. I'd like for you to start in the auditing department. You should be appropriately dressed in a suit and tie. You will work with the auditors learning something about how the system is organized.'

Then he turned to me and said, 'Mr. Tatum, you won't need a suit and tie because we are going to furnish you with an apron. You will start tomorrow morning at 6 working on the loading dock.'

At that time, I had a bachelor's degree in liberal arts from the University of Chicago and a master's in business administration from Loyola University. In addition, I had five years assistant management experience working for a public agency.

Despite my education and work experience, I worked on the dock and in the receiving room for about two months, wearing a small apron. They also furnished me with a knife for cutting boxes, rope and stuff. One evening, before I could get my foot in the front door, my wife greeted me with, 'You're nothing but a damn fool, down there burning boxes and operating a freight elevator. I think they are simply making a clown out of you.'

Needless to say, I did not sleep well that night. When I arrived at work the next morning, I called headquarters and spoke to the personnel guy that hired me. I told him things were not going too well because I was still working on the dock and in the receiving room.

In anger I blurted, 'I've learned about all I can learn about lifting, counting and receiving merchandise and looking up back orders.'

During the conversation I admitted that there was something to learn by working on the dock but it certainly should not take two months to do it.

The personnel man said, 'Cool down! When you hang up the phone, go to the store manager's office and just wait there.'

So I went directly to the manager's office and told the secretary that I wanted to see the manager. She told me that I didn't have an appointment. And the manager would let me know when he wanted to see me. I simply ignored the secretary's remarks and took a seat outside of the store manager's door.

In less than two minutes, the manager rushed out of the office. His face was as flushed as a red Wisconsin apple. Without even a greeting, he told me to report directly to the accounting office.

I finally crawled out of that branch and then hurdled barricade after barricade throughout the entire system until I hit the 'black summit,' which is middle management.

It's frustrating when I look back 25 years and compare my movement in the company with my white counterparts who started working for the company the same time that I did with less all-around working equipment other than the color of their skin. I found that there was a great disparity between the number of opportunities and job assignments my white counterparts were given as compared to those that I received. When the boss that you report to daily started a year after you did and is still moving up, and you have to acknowledge at middle age plus 10 that you have leveled off at a middle executive spot, you've got to either be angry or a fool.

As corporate America looks at itself in the mirror of the 1990s, it has to acknowledge that its 25-year experiment of including minorities and females in its top executive ranks has been a dismal failure. Corporate America opted to be white rather than right.

AMERICA'S CHOCOLATES
DON'T MELT

Mittie Travis, my mother, affectionately referred to me interchange-
ably as her sweet little chocolate man or her precious black velvet when
I was between the ages of three and five. Those endearing names
imbued me with a pleasurably exalted personal image. It was not until
after I celebrated my 7th birthday that I learned that my mother's little
chocolate man could not melt into the American cultural mainstream
like boys and girls of other ethnic origins.

My initial culture shock occurred when my cousin Frank and I
presented ourselves at the box office of the Oakland Square Theater on
Chicago's South Side at 39th and Drexel Blvd., on a Saturday afternoon.
It was on May 19, 1927, when the buxom theater cashier confronted us.
"Black boys are not admitted here. If you don't get away from in front
of this theater that burly blond, blue-eyed usher standing in the door
behind me will kick your little nigger behinds," she warned.

Frank and I took off for home like two scared rabbits chased by a
pack of salivating Mississippi bloodhounds. Although 63 years have
passed, the painful shock is as fresh today as any terrifying experience
that might have happened yesterday. The incident forced me to
become a firm believer in the theory that you may consciously forgive
but, subconsciously, you never forget.

The mental scars of racism inflicted upon me during my early years are mere scratches compared with the deep wounds suffered by the persons described in the following case study.

John Brown's parents were light-skinned. His mother could pass for a White Anglo Saxon Protestant (WASP), and his father's skin was several shades darker. Dr. Brown, had he chosen to affect a Spanish or Portuguese accent, could have easily been assimilated into the white world.

Johnny, who was blue-eyed and white-skinned like his mother, never sensed that the world was different for him until he was 6 years old. His rude awakening came in January 1945, near the end of World War II, when he entered the first grade at the A.O. Sexton Elementary School at 6020 S. Langley in Chicago. When he returned home after his first day in school, his mother asked: "What color is your teacher? Is she colored or white?"

"What are we?" Little Johnny queried.

His mother replied, "We are colored."

"The teacher is white," Johnny said.

Several days later, Johnny's mother visited Sexton school and discovered that the teacher was as Black as anthracite coal. The little boy's confusion was understandable: he observed that the teacher's skin color was the opposite of his mother's glistening white face and his own milky white hands. Since they were colored, he reasoned that his teacher must be white.

In the spring of 1947, Johnny's father, an engineer who taught at the University of Chicago, accepted a 4-month assignment in Hawaii. Throughout their ocean voyage, people asked Johnny and his brother Steve what nationality they were. By their second day at sea, the bombardment of questions about race caused Dr. Brown to erupt in anger. He commanded his two young sons to tell anyone who asked them about their nationality that they were Americans.

One elderly lady became a pain in the behind by asking the boys several times a day, "What race are you?" On their fourth day at sea, the boys made up something they thought would be incredible enough to staunch her inquisitiveness. They told the lady that they were one-sixth Greek, two-sixths Indian, one-twelveth Irish, and every other combination they could think of. The lady did not bother them with her nationality nonsense for the rest of the voyage.

Herb Jeffries, a vocalist with the Duke Ellington Orchestra, had the same experience as the Brown brothers seven years earlier. One night, in September 1940, a patron in a nightclub was sharing a table with a party that included Jeffries. After several rounds of drinks, one member of the party stared at Herb and blurted, "I assumed you were colored based on your recordings. But you aren't, are you?"

"What do you mean by colored?" Jeffries asked quietly.

"Why, anyone with Negro blood."

"How much Negro blood?" queried Jeffries.

"Any Negro blood, I guess," the man replied uneasily.

"Two drops?" retorted Jeffries.

The man nodded.

"It must be some mighty great stuff," the singer recoiled. "If, for instance, you had a black paint so powerful that two drops of it would color a bucket of white paint, that would be the most potent paint in the world. So if Negro blood is as strong as all that, it must be some mighty powerful stuff."

Jeffries was right about the potency of Black. In the fall of 1955, there was a news wire service story that stated that Black fullback Bobby Grier would sweat, bleed and probably elicit cheers on a Dixie football field. The story upset the people of the sovereign state of Georgia, riled sports circles around the world, and so clouded the mind of Gov. Marvin Griffin that even his race-baiting henchmen begged him to "grow up."

The young Brown brothers grew and matured so much as first graders that their parents enrolled them in the University of Chicago Laboratory School when they were promoted to the second grade. There was a handful of Black kids in their class plus a thumb and four fingers of Blacks who were one year ahead of them in their new school. Most of the children were sons and daughters of professionals and many, like the Brown brothers, were so light-skinned that they could pass for white. The brothers knew that 98 percent of the residents in their West Woodlawn neighborhood were Black, while in East Hyde Park, where most of the white students lived, all of the occupants, except the maids and yard men, were buttermilk white. Since their parents had friends among the Black and white races, and all of their father's colleagues at the university were white, the Brown children escaped the full impact of Jim Crow.

When he was in the sixth grade, Johnny was fairly popular among the children at the Lab School. He had lots of white friends, both male and female. At the beginning of the semester in seventh grade, he was invited to attend a dance at the home of a white classmate. That proved to be his last invitation to such occasions. He later found out that no other Black children were invited to parties given by their white classmates, and it took him a little while to get a fix on what was happening.

Although the Blacks at the Lab School were not invited to any parties, groups of white and Black students would go to the Hyde Park movie theaters on Saturday afternoons. As the sap rose in the spring, the students began pairing off into couples. Johnny asked several of the white girls in the group to be his date, but they turned him down. He didn't understand—he was tall, blond, blue-eyed and handsome by WASP standards. Suddenly, a light went on in his head one afternoon when one of the white girls he was pursuing for a date said, "You will have to talk to my mother."

Johnny told his mother, who called the girl's mother only to be told that she didn't want her daughter going out with a colored boy. It was a profound and sobering experience for the young Black when confronted with the fact that though he was popular in the classroom, he could not socialize with the white students after dark. The realization hit him with a stinging force more chilling than a January wind in Chicago.

Johnny's only recourse to avoid being devoured by hate and anger was to associate with a group of white non-athletic, not-too-bright classmates he called misfits. Today, some of them are counted among the avant garde in the business community and are known for not allowing race to become a barrier to friendships. Several of the students have become leaders in Fortune 500 companies.

After completing eighth grade, Johnny transferred to Hyde Park High School, where approximately 40 to 50 percent of the students were Black, 40 percent were Jewish and about 5 percent were Japanese. Johnny and his friends referred to Hyde Park High as Zebra Tech because the students embraced integrated socialization. The choir was integrated, the basketball team was integrated, the football team was integrated and the parties were integrated. White guys were going out with Black girls and Black guys were going out with white girls. The socialization drove their parents nuts: there was no way the Jewish parents could stop their kids from going to Black parties and there was no way that Black parents could stop their kids from going to Jewish parties.

Many friendships formed between the Browns and whites at Zebra Tech have survived until this day. When these old friends meet, their conversations are laced with talk about the uniqueness of the years from 1955 through 1959. They remember when Herbie Hancock, the now-famous pianist/composer, was elected king of Hyde Park High and became the first Black to attain that lofty status. Hancock's election showed Johnny that there wasn't anything wrong with being Black, that it was not his fault that he went from a popular person to a pariah at the University of Chicago Lab School. Almost immediately after transferring to Hyde Park High, just three blocks south of the Lab School, Johnny became a popular guy again.

Steve Brown left the Lab School a year after his brother Johnny because he encountered similar racial problems. He had become a reject and a punching bag for some of the white toughs. When Steve arrived at Hyde Park High, he rediscovered his outgoing personality and ability to function as a top-flight student, thus mirroring his brother's overnight transformation. The public high school was a three-block walk from 59th St. to 62nd and Stony Island, yet a completely different, much better world for Blacks of every hue.

Johnny didn't do too well academically at Hyde Park but he excelled in Popularity 101. For his senior year, his parents sent him to Kushon Academy, Ashburn Anne, Mass., an institution with a reputation for accepting a few Black students, with the purpose of preparing them for a college education.

When Johnny walked in the boys' dorm at Kushon, the 17-year-old Chicagoan didn't know a soul. The dorm was jammed with students engrossed in watching a baseball game on television involving the Milwaukee Braves. It might have been the World Series.

The first words that Johnny heard were, "Kill that coon!"

They were talking about Hank Aaron, who was up at bat. Johnny thought, "Well, if they're gonna kill Hank Aaron on TV, they're gonna kill me now because I'm right here with them." He was terrified. He heard racial references that he had never heard before: coon, jake, spade, tree climber. "Oh my God, what is going to happen to me?" he wondered.

The presence of his first cousin, James, who was lodged across the road in another dorm offered Johnny little comfort because they were the only two Black males in the school. Johnny was scared dungless, a reaction his mother anticipated he would have in a new environment more than a thousand miles from home. She had suggested that he take pictures of the family to keep on his dresser for those occasions when someone would come in and ask, "Well, who are these people?" Johnny could respond, "That's my family."

"Hopefully," his mother said, "they will get the message and you won't have to explain or wear a sign saying, 'I am a Negro.'" That proved to be a very effective antidote to Johnny's racial exclusivity.

Although he was at Kushon for just seven months, Johnny was elected the most popular person in his senior class; his cousin James ranked as the second-highest academic achiever at the school.

After graduating from Kushon Academy, Johnny went to Grinnell College, Grinnell, Iowa, which he described as "a piece of cake" because he encountered few racial problems during the four-year tenure. The only glimpse of racism occurred when he was initially assigned to a room with two other Blacks. When his father heard about it, he hit the ceiling and called the president of the college. "How could a progressive school put three colored kids in the same room?" Dr. Brown bellowed.

The boys were immediately switched to different quarters, but after spending one night with their new roommates, they decided they would rather room together. Thus, they became roomies, by choice, for the four years they were at Grinnell.

The college also attempted to match the three Black guys with three Black girls on the campus, but the guys paid the school's matchmaking efforts little to no attention. They dated white as well as Black girls, causing Johnny to describe Grinnell as "kind of an ideal world."

Law school proved to be a totally different environment from Johnny's Grinnell experience. He attended Northwestern Law School in Chicago, which he said, "was filled with absolute bigots." There are only two people from his class that Johnny maintains any communications with today.

Johnny recalls that when he enrolled at the law school, he filled out his application about race and religion honestly, and was assigned a single room at Abbott Hall on the downtown campus of Chicago's Northwestern University. The same treatment was given to Jewish students, who were either paired with other Jews or given a single room.

Johnny describes the demographics of the Northwestern law school student body as about one-third Chicago Irish-Catholic, one-third Chicago Jews and one-third WASP from around the country. Johnny recalls:

They were really a bad group of people. The law students were unlike any other students I had known, with their, 'We

don't like niggers,' attitude. Moreover, during my three
years at the law school, they never abandoned their dislike
for Blacks. It was a tough place. A lot of the Irish guys were
from the Gage Park area on the Southwest Side of Chicago.
We're talking about the early '60s, when civil rights issues
and Dr. Martin Luther King Jr. were in the forefront of the
news.

After the end of his first year at law school, Johnny said he had
"swallowed as much of the bigotry" as he could stomach without
regurgitating green liver bile in the middle of the lecture hall. The
situation was so unpleasant that he took every opportunity to leave
Abbott Hall for the sanctuary of home with his parents, who had
moved from West Woodlawn to Hyde Park. Johnny didn't fare very
well academically at the law school because he could not concentrate on
his studies in that racially charged environment. When he told his
father that if he didn't drop out, the school would put him out, Dr.
Brown asked, "Don't you know any members of the faculty? Don't you
know any students?"

Johnny replied, "I just can't stand it. Dad, you can't imagine how
awful it is." It was a devastating confession for the young man who had
been the most popular person in his senior class at the Kushon
Academy and twice was elected class president at Grinnell College.

Johnny insisted that he was going to drop out, but his father
stomped his foot down on the living room floor and screamed: "There
must be somebody that you can talk to."

After some thought, Johnny remembered John Kaplan, his professor in a real estate law course. Kaplan was a mild-mannered man who
had displayed a real sense of humor. In addition, Kaplan had written a
report on desegregating New Rochelle, N.Y., for the Civil Rights
Commission on Housing, and Johnny reasoned Kaplan's ethnicity and
experience might have given him some empathy for another minority.

Brown was on the mark because Kaplan told Johnny that dropping
out of law school would be a big mistake. "I'm sure you've taken note on
the idiots around here," he told Johnny. "These are the dumbest people
I've ever taught. There is no reason that you can't do the work better
than they can. I know that you're smarter than nine-tenths of them,
and I'm telling you to stay in school. I will see that the professors in
each of your classes gives you some attention."

Johnny moved back into Abbott Hall at North Lake Shore Drive and Chicago Avenue. Kaplan kept his promise and Johnny's grades improved dramatically.

In his third and last year in law school, Johnny Brown assembled a resume that included his activities with the Black Law Students' Alliance.

Johnny recalls his first interview with a major corporation in Detroit. He had already been interviewed by two officers of the firm, and things were going great. He felt that he had the job in the bag. The third member of the firm's interview team looked at Johnny's resume and came to a dead halt when he reached the section on student activities. He looked at Johnny and glanced back at the resume several times before continuing the conversation. Brown recalls the following question and answer session:

"Johnny, what is the Black Law Students' Alliance?" the corporate counselor asked.

"It's an organization of Black law students at my law school," Johnny replied.

"Well, I've got a couple of more questions for you," the interviewer said. "Number one, why do Blacks need an alliance like this to begin with?"

"It's somewhat of a support group for each of us," Johnny retorted. "Our law school doesn't have a great number of minority students to begin with. The Black Law Students' Alliance is kind of a social group and also kind of a close knit support group."

"I don't understand why Blacks would need their own separate group," the lawyer said.

Johnny replied, "For many years Blacks have had to have their separate groups because they weren't allowed in majority groups. For example, for years the American Bar Association and the Chicago Bar Association did not permit any Blacks to become members."

Johnny had anticipated the next question. "Why are you in the group?" the corporate counselor asked.

"What do you mean why am I in that group?" Johnny responded.

"I don't understand how you got in the group," the counselor replied.

"What do you mean you don't understand how I got in the group?" Johnny retorted.

"Did they have some special type of admissions policy or were you just simply voted in?" queried the corporate counselor.

Johnny decided that he was not going to let the man off the hook. "I decided I would make him ask me point blank. Finally, after a group of idiotic questions that you wouldn't expect from a lawyer in a major corporation, he finally asked, 'Are you Black?' "

"What difference does it make?" Johnny snapped. "Don't you know it's unlawful to ask about race? What is the purpose of you asking that question?"

The counselor softly replied, "I'm just trying to figure out how you got into the organization."

Johnny decided he wasn't going to waste more time playing hide-and-seek on the race issue. "Yes, I am Black," Brown blurted out. "And that's why I'm a member of the organization."

The corporation counselor's face became as red as a Santa Claus suit. From that point, the interview went downhill.

Johnny said, "I knew when I prepared the resume that if I omitted putting in the fact that I was affiliated with the Black Law Students' Alliance I could have gotten a number of jobs and passed myself off as a white boy. But I have selected not to live a lie." Conversely, Congress-man Adam Clayton Powell, D-N.Y., passed for white and joined a white fraternity while a student at Colgate University.

Brown was too culturally Black to be white, and too physically white to be considered Black sans a tag. He felt that his white skin disqualified him from being Black enough to serve as the African American token in a white law firm.

In contrast to the Johnny Brown cat-and-mouse interview, the recruiter who, in the fall of 1988, interviewed Linda Golden, a Black third-year law student at the University of Chicago, was blatantly racist.

Harry O'Kane, partner and recruiter for Baker and McKenzie, a major law firm with 31 offices outside of the United States, asked Ms. Golden how she would respond if she were called a "Black bitch" or a "nigger" by a legal adversary.

Later in the interview, when Ms. Golden told Mr. O'Kane that she played golf, he responded, "Why don't Blacks have their own country club?" Without waiting for a reply, he continued, "The reason Blacks don't have country clubs is that there aren't too many golf courses in the ghetto."

"Jews have their own country clubs," he added. "I never wanted to belong to a Jewish country club, but at least they have their own."

The law firm of Baker and McKenzie was barred from recruiting on the University of Chicago campus for a year as a result of students' complaints of racist, sexist and anti-Semitic slurs by Mr. O'Kane.

A federal recruiter came to the rescue of Johnny Brown. He was actively recruiting qualified minorities regardless of their sex or the shade of complexion. Thus, Johnny landed his first legal job working for a government body in the District of Columbia. Johnny's white complexion triggered some very interesting experiences during his tour with the U.S. government. One day during a fire drill, a Black secretary ran up to Johnny as he stood in line: "Do you mind if I ask you a question?"

Johnny replied, "Go ahead."

"There is a rumor going around that you are Black," the secretary said.

Johnny retorted, "I don't know why there is a rumor going around that I'm Black because I am Black."

The secretary replied, "Oh my gosh. They never knew that."

"What do you mean, they never knew?"

She said, "I'm certain that most of the lawyers working in this agency don't know that you're Black."

Johnny could not figure out why the rumor existed—the people that he socialized with during and after work were Black, as were his daily luncheon companions.

All sorts of nonsense seeps into the ears of Blacks who appear to be white. For example, when Johnny was trying a case in the state of Washington, a Black witness said, "The judge is trying to figure out who you are. He knows that you are from Chicago. Beyond that, he doesn't know ethnically what you are and that's causing him a lot of trouble."

Johnny told the witness:

I think I understand the judge's problem because almost everyone in the United States from the president to the federal judiciary to Joe and Mary Citizen sitting in the jury box holds a certain personal bias. The bias may focus on age or the sex of an individual, or even certain sections of the country that some people call home. But the overriding prejudice is directed at race. Every individual—lawyer, judge or whoever—brings a personal bias into the picture when following a profession or deciding who is going to marry their daughters or sons. That shouldn't be, but it is.

Between 1932 and 1952, more than 5 million white-complexioned Negroes chose to make a complete transformation from the Black world into the white world. During the two decades, thousands more tried living in two worlds, passing as white during the day to find and hold decent paying white-collar jobs and returning to their Negro neighborhoods at night. The dual lifestyles locked them into a Jekyll-Hyde conflict between their day world and their night world. It was a stressful existence to know that some of their white friends would be shocked to learn of their Negro blood and that many of their Negro friends would look upon them with scorn for denying their heritage, despite the fact that they passed for white only to obtain and retain employment.

One girl who passed for white to get work as a clerk in the Marshall Field's department store in the Chicago's Loop thought she had lost her job when a well-meaning friend of her mother's came into the store and almost broke her neck during a double take. "Well, baby, it's sure good to see this store is finally hiring colored girls," she said in a happy surprised voice. Fortunately, the woman was overheard by only one person, a white clerk who was a good friend of the saleswoman and kept her secret.

A young woman, a Harvard graduate who passed in order to hold an administrative position with a large white-owned firm, said, "I'm not ashamed of my race. If I could be Black and still hold this job, I'd let everyone know right now." Her attitude captured the sentiment of the hundreds of thousands of workers who in 1990 are white by day and Black by night. A 1987 report from the U.S. Bureau of Census indicates the racial crossovers that could occur in the next century: 100,000 children of mixed parentage were born in the United States in 1987, compared with 30,000 born in 1968. Both sons of Supreme Court Justice Thurgood Marshall are products of a mixed marriage who have crossed over and married white women.

Actress Jennifer Beal was born in Chicago in 1963. Her mother Jeanne is Irish and her Black father Alfred was the prosperous owner of several South Side Chicago grocery stores. Alfred died in 1974 and Jeanne, a schoolteacher, moved her family to an all-white North Side community. From that day to the present, Jennifer has never publicly identified with the Black community. In contrast, Jasmine Guy, the female lead in Eddie Murphy's "Harlem Nights" and a star in Bill Cosby's television hit, "A Different World," is the product of a biracial marriage who has always presented herself as Black. At the other extreme, Prince, whose parents are Black, claims in his publicity that he is Italian.

America's chocolates don't melt, and neither do the marshmellows who have chocolate inside.

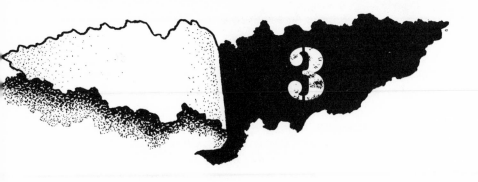

YOU MAY BE PRESIDENT, BUT YOU ARE STILL A NIGGER

Franklin Madison was born in 1949 in Romeoville, a small rural town in central Ohio. The Baltimore and Ohio Railroad tracks that ran through the middle of the town served as a racial dividing line. All the Blacks in Romeoville lived on the south side of the B & O tracks and their living conditions were four grades below poor. The sidewalks and roads on the Black side of town were unpaved. Although the country was in the second half of the 20th century, street lights and sewer drainage had not reached the colored section of town, while the white folks who lived in big houses within 200 feet across the B & O tracks, enjoyed inside plumbing, paved sidewalks and thoroughfares drenched in bright lights.

As a child, Franklin frequently stared across the tracks in awe of the lifestyles that whites enjoyed, yet he does not recall feeling deprived. Even today, as he gazes out of the large picture window of his $650,000 home in a 99.9 percent white-populated Cincinnati suburb, he retains rich memories of his childhood when he lived on the south side of the track.

There was only one school in Romeoville, and the Black kids were forced to take a single designated path through the white section of town to reach the school. Any youngster who strayed from that path

23

would be stopped by a white person or a law enforcement official and told, "Go home or go to school. You don't belong in the white section of town."

The racism that prevailed in Romeoville in the 1950s is a paradox when you consider that 100 years earlier, Ohio was one of the layovers for runaway slaves enroute to Canada seeking refuge via Harriet Tubman's underground railroad. Another incongruity for Romeoville Blacks was the busing of white children to a school, that, in some instances, was less than a mile from their homes while Black students were forced to walk across town. There were no yellow school buses for little Black boys and girls.

Franklin Madison recalls:

I never could understand nor accept the basic tenents of racism. My parents never acted in a fashion that made any of their five children feel inferior because of the color of our skin. I can remember third grade as if it were yesterday. I was very gregarious and outgoing, a good student, a good athlete and well-liked. My school friends lived on both sides of the B & O railroad tracks.

One day, I walked through the school corridors and I saw Ken O'Donnell, one of my friends, in a huddle with some other whites who were prompting him to accost me. Ken acquiesced to his buddies' wishes to prove that he was not a nigger lover. He came over and pushed me and invited me to come outside into the schoolyard. 'Why are you doing this?' I asked. 'We are friends.'

Ken did not say a word, he just continued to push and shove me around while his white buddies egged him on. They were concerned that O'Donnell had appeared to be a better friend to me than he was to them.

Finally, I became angry and started to tussle. I wrestled him to the ground and got the best of him by pinning his arms and shoulders down with both of my legs. Realizing that he couldn't even move, Ken looked up at me with a Dracular-like glare in his tearing eyes and said, 'You may have kicked my ass, but you're still a nigger.'

That profound statement about our society came out of the mouth of a 7-year-old white kid who was getting his tail whipped in front of his friends. Ken obviously felt that the only thing that's worse than being beaten by a Black in a fight was to be Black.

Between the third grade in elementary school and my senior year in high school, I suffered several personal affronts because of my Blackness. The one that stands out even more than my schoolyard fight with my former white childhood friend took place when I was a senior in high school.

The school population of Romeoville High was roughly 20 percent Black and 80 percent white. I was a top student in my class and one of the state's best high school athletes. I was selected to be captain of the football team in my senior year. There were no problems until we started preparing for homecoming.

As the captain of the football team I was to crown the queen at the homecoming game and give her a kiss on the cheek, a ritual which had been part of the homecoming ceremonies for 40 or 50 years.

About a month before homecoming, kids started asking me, 'What are you gonna do this year? Are you gonna kiss the queen?'

I said, 'Yea, that's the way it works.'

My response started a lot of conversations around the school because the queen and all of the girls in her court were white. The talk about a Black boy kissing the white homecoming queen was not confined to students; it served as the main course during breakfast and lunch among the school's teachers and administrators.

Two weeks before homecoming, Principal Roger Cahill called me into his office.

'Franklin,' he said, 'there's a lot of conversation about you crowning the queen. We really think that you're a great kid—great for the school. We all know you're going to go places in life, but we are faced with a situation everybody's talking about. We've never had this problem before. We've never had a colored football captain. I'm not sure how the community's going to respond if you crown the queen and kiss her.'

After pausing for a few moments, Franklin replied, "The kiss is ceremonial and it's been a part of the tradition. I'm simply gonna kiss the queen on her right cheek. If anybody's got a problem with that, I don't understand why."

The principal retorted, "Well, Franklin, it has nothing to do with you. It's just that a lot of people are narrow-minded and they can't quite think through some things. I'd like to know if you seriously plan on kissing the queen."

"Well, I'll tell you," Franklin said, "I feel like I'm entitled to do that. But right now I don't know."

The principal recoiled, "Well! I need to have you promise me that you won't do it."

"I can't make that promise! I don't know!" Franklin sputtered. "It's my time to crown the queen and kiss her. I have that right because of my position as captain of the football team."

Principal Cahill bellowed, "If you don't promise me, we're going to have to take some action."

"What action?" young Franklin asked.

Cahill repeated, "If you don't promise me, I'll take some action."

Franklin abruptly executed a drill sergeant's about-face and stormed out of the principal's office.

Principal Cahill cancelled the homecoming parade and ceremonies the next morning. Racism had deprived Franklin Madison of his day in the sun and deprived the entire school of enjoying its annual tradition.

The reason the principal gave for cancelling the ceremonies was a lot of gobbledygook. The assistant principal attempted to pacify Franklin with some nonsense about an inability to resolve the parade logistics. The lies perplexed and angered the young man.

The homecoming controversy spilled across the Baltimore and Ohio railroad tracks into the Black community where the people put two and two together and got seven. The whole matter began to smell to them like rancid racism, and the Franklin Madison affair fostered multiple layers of hatred between Black and white folk thick enough to cut with a knife.

The week before homecoming, Franklin broke his ankle and was unable to play football for the rest of the season. Like a bolt out of the blue, the school administrators resolved the fabricated parade logistics problem, hastily rescheduled the homecoming parade and homecoming queen-crowning ceremony, and appointed a white football captain. Although Franklin was on the sidelines with a cast on his leg, there was no legitimate reason why he could not have crowned and kissed the homecoming queen.

During halftime ceremonies just moments before the captain-designate was to crown the queen, a fight broke out between some whites and Blacks in the grandstand. The ill will that had been building up before the game had popped off like an overheated radiator cap. During the commotion, the queen's court was pushed into several cars and rushed out of the stadium, and the crowning never occurred. After more than an hour, the police finally got the disturbance under control. School authorities, following the advice of the police, cancelled the homecoming dance because they feared that the fighting would be renewed and more people would get hurt.

Franklin ended his high school athletic career as a good, not great, football player because of the broken ankle. However, he was offered several full basketball scholarships and a number of academic scholarships. He accepted a basketball offer from Ohio State University in Columbus.

Franklin had been advised because of good mathematics skills to major in engineering. Thus, his first act upon reaching the Ohio State campus was to register. He then proceeded from registration to the gym, where he was greeted by the coach-recruiter, who said: "Franklin, you're gonna have to go over and get registered."

"I've already registered sir," Franklin replied.

The coach said, "Well, did you talk to the athletic academic advisor?"

Franklin replied, "Oh, I didn't know we had one."

"Yeah, you need to go down and talk to him right away," the coach said.

Franklin thought that this was a great idea because the academic advisor would help him sort through this maze of courses that he had already signed up for. The next morning, he met with the advisor to discuss his course load and the possibility of obtaining employment on campus.

"I understand you've registered already," the academic advisor began.

"Yes sir," Franklin replied.

The advisor responded, "I'd like to see your registration slip."

When Franklin gave it to him, the advisor's lower jaw dropped almost to his navel. "You signed up for all of these courses?" he mumbled.

"That's right, sir!"

With an unlit cigar dangling out of the right side of his mouth, the advisor asked, "Who the hell do you think you are?"

With a surprised look on his face, young Madison responded, "Pardon me?"

"I said who in the hell do you think you are? How do you think you can play basketball and take these heavyweight courses?"

"Sir, those are the courses that I have to take if I want to get a degree in the field that I am interested in," Franklin retorted.

The advisor slammed his ham-sized fist down on his rolltop desk and said, "You can't take those courses. No way. Organic chemistry. Calculus. You just can't take those courses. Did you come here to be a student or an athlete? If you want to play basketball at Ohio State, you're gonna take the courses I recommend."

The advisor tore up Franklin's registration slip and threw it in the trash can. He then pulled out a new registration slip, filled it out and told Franklin, "These are the courses that you're gonna take."

The first course on the new registration slip was basketball. Since Franklin was on a basketball scholarship, he said, "You want me to take basketball and I'm on a basketball scholarship? It doesn't make sense. That's a waste of my time and a waste of the university's money."

The professor looked at Franklin and said, "We know that you're going to be able to pass that course."

The other courses were equally as ridiculous and unrelated to Franklin's engineering dream and no consideration was given to his high school academic record. It was obvious that the advisor had not looked at Franklin's high school transcript, he had simply glanced at him and said to himself, "You are a Black jock and capable of only passing Mickey Mouse courses."

Franklin recognized that the academic advisor harbored a stereotypical perception of him. After the professor processed the course changes, Franklin reinstated his original registration. When the coach learned about Franklin's actions, he was so irate that he threatened to throw his uppity behind off of the basketball team.

Franklin made his case with the advisor and the coach when he convinced them that he came to Ohio State University to learn something as well as to contribute to the basketball team. "I think I can do both. In fact, if I get to the point where my grades preclude me from playing basketball, then I will listen to you. But I deserve the right to pursue both objectives because I don't see them as mutually exclusive."

Franklin achieved his objectives. He graduated from the college of engineering in four years, and also played on the first string of the basketball team for the entire four years he was at Ohio State.

A survey taken in 1989 by the senate's Labor and Human Resources Committee, chaired by Sen. Edward M. Kennedy, D-Mass.,
revealed that 35 of the 97 schools reported graduation ratios of 0 to 20
percent for their basketball players. The graduation ratio for football
players was only a little better. In contrast, 162 of the 175 students who
entered Stanford University in Palo Alto, Calif., in 1982 graduated. At
Duke University, Durham, N.C., 42 of 42 varsity basketball players
enrolled since 1975 have graduated.

Franklin Madison endured a lonely existence while attending Ohio
State—he was a strange fruit because he was the only Black in the
engineering school and he was also a jock. The professors who thought
Franklin should not have been both an engineering student and an
athlete kept the pressure on him. For example, if a test was scheduled
for Friday and he was scheduled to leave on Wednesday before the
examination to go on the road with the basketball team, Franklin
would have to take the test before going on the road. The tight ship
they forced on him would have broken the spirit of most men, but
instead it instilled discipline in Franklin and afforded him with some
insight into how to use racism as a honing device for sharpening the
skills that he would later need to get ahead in corporate America.

Blacks in corporate America must be twice as well disciplined as
their white counterparts, Franklin learned during his four years at
Ohio State. In his first year, he was a summer intern at General Motors
and during his sophomore year he interned at Ford Motor Company.
During these summer internships, he found out the hard way that for
most people opportunity does not knock twice because on two occasions he procrastinated and lost opportunities for advancement.

During his junior and senior years, Franklin accepted an internship at the XYZ Company in Pennsylvania. He continued to work
there after graduation and found each promotion challenging and
rewarding. After working for the company for two years, he was asked
to relocate to a new plant in Alabama where he would manage a
start-up team.

Franklin recalled:

It wasn't an easy decision to go to Alabama because in 1973
it was still viewed as a highly racist state. However, the
company adopted a philosophy designed for the good of the
community specifically and of the South generally.

Management went on record that their policy of paying Blacks, whites and browns the same wages for the same work and responsibility would be the standard operating principle for the Alabama plant.

The company also agreed to a hiring formula based on a percentage of the population mix. In this particular area of Alabama the Black population was 40 percent.

Before going down to Alabama, I heard reports at company headquarters that, in spite of the incentives, Blacks were not showing up at the personnel office in Alabama for interviews. The undercurrent was that Blacks simply preferred to collect a welfare check rather than go to work. Some of the company officials actually thought it was a mistake to set such high goals for the employment of Blacks. Some went so far as to say that if the company accepted everybody who showed up for work, no more than five Blacks would be hired because so few had applied.

Franklin was perplexed. Although he didn't know anything about Alabama, he couldn't believe Blacks in that state were ignoring an opportunity to interview for work. His instincts were verified when he arrived in Alabama.

I had to wear my Saturday backyard work clothes on my first day on the job in Alabama, so I didn't look like the white-collar management type. As I drove to the plant, I listened to the Black radio station tell about the XYZ Company building a plant in Zero, Ala., and that comparable wages would be paid to Blacks and whites who worked there. The station encouraged Blacks to submit applications and be interviewed for employment at XYZ Company.

When Franklin arrived at the plant site he found only mobile offices, a guard house and a cyclone fence enclosing the property. Two guards came out of the guard house when Franklin pulled up to the gate. One guard went around the car to the passenger side and the other approached him on the driver side. Franklin noticed that both guards wore sidearms, and wondered why.

The guard on the driver's side of the car motioned to me to lower my window. As I started to lower it, the guard said,

'What are you doing here boy?'

'Pardon me?'

'Turn this car around and get the hell out of here nigger,' the guard said.

I replied, 'I don't understand. I just heard an advertisement that said XYZ Company was interviewing applicants for jobs. Is this the XYZ plant?'

'Nigger, I said turn this car around and get the hell out of here. It's none of your Black ass business what the name of this company is.'

I persisted: 'I need to know if this is the XYZ facility.'

The guard repeated, 'If you don't turn this car around and get the hell out of here, your people may not ever hear from you again.'

By this time, the other guard pulled his gun out of the holster and began to fondle it in a manner that let me know he was not bashful about using it. 'If you are trying to intimidate me, it's working,' I told him.

He said, 'Turn this car around boy, right now.'

'I will do that, but my boss is gonna be very upset,' I replied.

'What do you mean?'

I said, 'I am down here from Pennsylvania. I'm a manager for XYZ Company, and I'm supposed to start to work today, but I'm gonna leave like you said. And I'm going right up the road to the phone booth and make a call to see if we can get to the bottom of this.'

'You work for XYZ Company?' the guard barked in an incredulous tone.

'Yes, I do. And if you tell your partner to put his gun away, I will reach into my hip pocket and get my ID,' I replied.

'Joe, put your gun up. Let me see your ID,' the guard demanded.

I showed him my XYZ ID and he said, 'Oh, Mr. Madison, I hope you don't misunderstand or misinterpret what we're doing here, sir! We are just trying to keep out the undesirables. I hope you understand that we're working to protect the XYZ Company's interest.'

I said, 'I understand. I understand very well. May I go through now?'

He said, 'Oh yes, sir! I hope Mr. Madison, you recognize that our actions had nothing to do with you at all.'

'I think I understand,' I assured him.

He said, 'No you don't. You're from the North and you don't understand how things work down here. Believe me, we are protecting your interest.'

I said, 'Yes, I understand very well,' and I sped up to the mobile office where I met my new boss for the first time.

Mr. David Cartright was sitting behind his desk when I introduced myself. After exchanging pleasantries, I asked my boss to go back to the guard house with me.

On the way, I told him what had transpired.

When we reached the guard house, the two guards were understandably concerned. I told them that they were fired and to get off the premises. I didn't know if I had the authority, but I did it, and it stuck. My boss backed me.

It was a rewarding feeling. It wasn't so much the seven-minute confrontation that I had with the guards, it was negating the notion that Black folks didn't want to work, and realizing that, unfortunately, no one in Pennsylvania had bothered to ask whether Blacks could enter unchallenged through the gates of the Alabama plant.

After working several years in Alabama as a manager, I was promoted to vice president of XYZ and returned to the Pennsylvania headquarters. My new position paid almost twice as much as I had made in Alabama plus all of the perks that belong to the vice president of a major corporation.

One of the perks was the use of a private company airplane. I reserved the plane one day because I had to make three stops in three different states and return to headquarters that night. I arrived at the air field 15 minutes early that bright sunny morning, boarded the plane and introduced myself as Mr. Madison. The pilot acknowledged my presence and I sat down, waiting for the plane to take off.

At 8:00 a.m., we were supposed to taxi off, but at 8:05 we were still sitting there. At 8:15 I got up and I knocked on the pilot's door. When he opened it, I asked, 'What is the problem?'

'Oh, we're waiting for Mr. Madison,' he replied.

I said, 'I'm Mr. Madison.'

'You're Mr. Madison?'

'Yes.'

'But we're waiting on vice president Madison.'

'I am vice president Madison.' When the pilot realized I was the company official he'd been waiting for, he became very embarrassed. 'Sorry, no problem,' he sputtered, and the plane took off promptly into the wild blue yonder.

The mindset of the pilot simply mirrored the racial IQ of the typical white American. Attitudes will not change until corporate America recognizes that yo-yo tokenism is a mere indulgence, subject to being jerked back at any given moment. Tokenism must be recognized as a milder form of racism and racism is like rain: if it's not falling in your location, it's gathering force somewhere nearby.

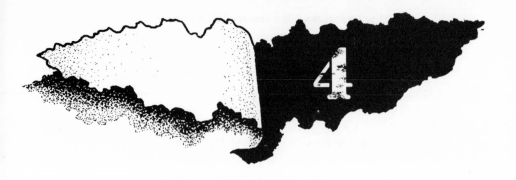

I PLAY LACROSSE.
WHO AM I?

The corridors of corporate America are teeming with highly trained Black men and women wandering trancelike through the monuments of commerce asking themselves, "Who am I?" The "Who am I" affliction is caused by the pervasive inequities of racism exhibited in the white corporate structure.

To lift yourself out of the depths of the corporate hole and rise to the top, you must thoroughly understand both the formal and informal structure. You may acquire an acquaintance with the formal corporate structure through courses at academic institutions, but the only way to learn the rules of the informal structure is through mentoring and the old boys' network.

If you are a Black determined to run on the fast track, you must be adopted by a "great white father" and plugged into lunch time or after-hour office politics. A Wednesday afternoon golf game with some senior executives, an occasional dinner at the boss' house, or a cocktail set after work with a corporate "mover and shaker" is a possible glory road to corporate heaven. Failure to be angelized and plugged into the system could possibly relegate you to the "Who am I" damnation for life.

Some of the ramifications of the "Who am I" malady were brought to my attention by several interviewees.

Vince Knight has a bachelor's degree in liberal arts from Yale University and is a graduate of the Harvard Graduate School of Business Administration. Vince and Charles Walker were classmates at both schools and both were employed by the same Fortune 500 company after graduation. However, Vince and Charles used different stepladders in their climb toward the glass ceiling that stifles the efforts of Blacks who aspire to reach for the top of the corporate ladder.

Their paths diverged when Charles adopted the persona of "them" and buried the "me." Vince and Charles were having lunch one day in the dining room used by middle management executives when, out of the clear blue sky, Chuck suddenly blurted out: "Yale was really a fine school before the Blacks got there. They have destroyed the genteel environment of the campus."

Vince craned his neck to find the person Charles was addressing in this strange manner. After all, Vince and Chuck were undeniably Black. It was then that Vince perceived that his troubled friend had subconciously denied his ethnicity to the extent that he had come to think of Vince and himself as white.

Vince, unlike Charles, prided himself in being anchored to the real world. He knew he would never be a part of the informal corporate structure and was even more certain that he would never be chairman or chief executive officer of a Fortune 500 company, despite his potential. Moreover, Vince resolved to keep his mental wheels intact by always holding one finger near the down button on the corporate elevator.

Charles had sacrificed his Black pride and ethnic parachute in a pathetic effort to join the White Anglo Saxon Protestant fraternity. He became skilled at playing lacrosse, tennis and squash, after deciding that those sports were to upper-class white males what basketball, baseball and football were to Blacks. But Charles' efforts made him a laughing stock among the whites he most admired. Many of those he tried to imitate disdainfully labeled Chuck as "whiter than white."

Charles culturally sold his soul but his aborted ethnic transformation backfired; he was ultimately fired because of poor job performance. Chuck is perhaps wondering, "If I had played the game my way instead of theirs, if I had not sold my soul, what might have happened?"

Vince, who is still employed by DBW Co., tells how he is constantly faced with the reality of his Blackness:

Every single day, I work harder than anyone else. I work longer and I am committed to getting the job done. I can't afford to mess up. If a white manager goofs, his supervisor is more than likely to say, 'We all make errors sometimes.' However, if I make the same mistake, the boss writes in his mental diary, 'I knew Vince could not perform the task. He is Black, and incompetent.'

I work to simply survive because there are no Black presidents or CEOs in my future. It's not because Blacks are not qualified to be presidents and chief executive officers of large corporations. We simply reach the glass ceiling and fade away faster than old movie stars.

The glass ceiling is crystallized racism, which has been institutionalized by the captains of industry.

Racism is so potent that it too frequently causes the victims to question their sanity. Colliding with racism is as mind-scrambling as having a brick thrown through your windshield when you're driving on an expressway.

When Blacks manage to slip through the corporate iron curtains that are guarded by the hawks of racism, then low- and middle-management people turn the 'white ants' loose on them. One of my ants is a bigoted white secretary who also works for two other executives. She lives in the Bridgeport area of Chicago. She's an ardent fan of the Black Hawk hockey team. The woman gets her kicks observing violence. When she was assigned to work for me, she didn't say, 'I'm not gonna work for you because you're Black.' Such a statement would have gotten her fired. However, when I tell her to do something, she simply sighs, rolls her eyes, frowns and stomps off to half-perform the task.

Her attitude is further reflected in the way she answers the phones. When she answers telephones for the other managers, she says, 'This is Mr. Blank Blank's office.' When she answers for me, she says, 'This is Vince's office.' When I ask her to answer my phone properly, she says, 'If you insist, I will,' and storms out of my space.

These racist tactics make an ordinary job difficult and sometimes impossible. If I misspell a word or make a grammatical error, my secretary—rather than correct it— leaves the mistake alone to make me look bad.

Beyond having the white ants nibbling away at the fibers of my soul, my greatest pressure comes with trying to determine how involved I must get with white folks away from the job. I think I wrestle with the perplexity of racial intermixing more often than any other single thing. The problem with getting involved with white managers is my recognition of our cultural differences. If I commit too much of my time and energy with them, I think of it as a sacrifice for something that I would rather do.

If I don't enjoy playing golf or other pastimes favored by white colleagues, but I feel that I need to learn how to play the game in order to interact with them, to me that's a sacrifice.

I don't drink. If they want to go out and get drunk and feel it's important for me to go out with them and get drunk, that would be an even greater sacrifice to me.

Many Blacks in the corporate environment decide early on that they're not gonna have anything to do with whites and create their own circle. There are some Blacks who are determined to be socially acceptable to whites, but whites don't recognize that these changes are considered as sacrifices by their Black co-workers. I have seen Blacks in white environments, obviously ill at ease, thinking to themselves, 'This is face time.' I refuse to do any face time.

I say I don't need to do face time because I've been around whites for a long time, both at the universities I attended and during my 10 years in the corporate jungle. If I had not graduated from prestigious universities, but instead attended "X" Black college and "X" Black graduate business school and then worked for a non-profit organization and shown up for my job, they would be alien to me. I can sympathize with those Blacks who must make that decision about face time.

On the other hand, there are some things where the interests of Blacks and whites overlap. I happen to like to play basketball, so when I play basketball with white colleagues on Wednesday night, that's not a sacrifice for me. I interact with them as peers on the court.

I don't really care what decision or what compromise a Black person might decide to make in order to put in face time. The only thing I say is that he or she must be able to internally justify whatever they do. That is, they should be able to sit down alone and say, I understand why I am doing this.

In contrast to Vince Knight's Ivy League background, Betty Dole was a graduate of Roosevelt University, an urban commuter school located in downtown Chicago. She did not know how to play tennis or golf, but she made up for that corporate deficit with superior intellect and a great deal of street smarts. She understood the need to interface with white folks and used it to her advantage as an account representative for a Fortune 500 manufacturing corporation.

Betty learned that to survive in the corporate world she would have to learn how to play the game by the white rules. The company she worked for sponsored annual golf and tennis tournaments. Since she was not interested in learning to golf, Betty took a tennis course from a pro and learned to play.

The company Betty worked for also counted their social functions as possible ladders to promotions, and held memberships in private clubs throughout metropolitan Chicago. Every year, the company hosted a night at Ravinia for staff, customers and their spouses to enjoy a concert and dinner served with candlelight and champagne.

Betty's job also included wining and dining her customers and attending the opera and theater with them at company expense. If her monthly expense sheets had failed to show that she had spent some time with the clients, her boss would figure that she had neglected important duties.

Cold calling on companies in Skokie, Schaumburg, Elk Grove Village, Elgin and other suburbs held definite advantages for a Black female. There was no way that the officers could forget Betty when she called back. Since several white manufacturing representatives called on those purchasing officers every day, Betty stood out like a fly floating on the top of a glass of sweet milk.

In spite of Betty's high profile advantage, her marketing career was not all peaches and cream:

One day the vice president of our company called me into the office and told me that he had assigned me to one of our conglomerate accounts. He said he wanted me to join him at lunch with the president, the treasurer and the purchasing agent of the new account. He called the president of the other company and told him that he was bringing me out for lunch so the president could be introduced to his new account executive, Betty Dole.

My boss later told me that the CEO repeated my name, paused and then said, 'Oh, my lord, we're getting a female.' He then went into a tirade of why it was not necessary to replace the old account executive with a female. He wanted to know if there was something wrong with the relationship between the two companies and so forth.

My vice president indicated that they were bringing me in because I was one of the brightest among the young account representatives and he thought it would benefit both companies if I serviced the account. 'Before you come to a conclusion, I think you ought to meet her,' he said. 'Incidently, I must also tell you that Betty is Black.'

A sudden silence followed as I watched my boss' face signal the storm brewing on the other end of the line.

After the vice president hung up the phone, he sighed, 'You don't have to go through with this lunch if you don't want to, but I think you should. This is something that our company is going to have to face sooner or later, I think we should face it now.'

I said fine and we went out to the Glenview Country Club. The account's chief executive officer asked me numerous questions about my background—where I went to school and other foolishness that had nothing to do with my ability to handle the account. Just before the dessert was served, we briefly discussed the relationship between the companies. I was prepared for him because I had done my homework on this account.

As we were leaving the dining room, the CEO suggested to my boss that he would like to drive me back to our office in his car so we could talk further. He asked me if I would mind riding with him and I said no.

When we got in his car, he said, 'I owe you an apology, Betty. You probably don't know why I'm saying this.'

I said, 'No, I don't,' although I did.

'When Frank called me and told me he was putting a female on the account, I want to tell you in no uncertain terms that I pitched a fit,' he confessed. 'Then when he said not only is she female but she is Black, I pitched a royal fit. However, Frank, to his credit, told me where I could take the account and stick it if I wanted to. And he was firm in his conviction in keeping you on the account. For that I give him a lot of credit. I feel that I owe you an apology because, first of all, I made a decision about you without ever having met you and learning of your qualifications. There's also the fact that your company has never hired any shoddy people in their shop. I owe you an apology and I hope you'll accept it. I'm glad that you're on our account.'

Betty became the superstar within a year after landing that account. Her next move up the corporate ladder would make her a line officer in head-to-head competition with white male peers. When the possibility of that promotion became a reality, all hell broke loose. Betty explains:

That company not only had never had a single Black officer, but had never even considered it. No Black stayed there long enough to become a vice president or a line officer. At that level you are managing other people, which, in my case, meant white males, and sitting on committees evaluating the performance of others. Officers of that company received such perks as membership in the Chicago Club, Union League Club, the Standard Club, the Cliff Dwellers Club, Mid America Club, the University Club and other private clubs. At that time, those organizations weren't admitting women in any of those establishments, even as a luncheon guest of a member. My bosses never contemplated the ramifications of a Black female becoming a vice president because they never imagined promoting a Black person or a female, white or otherwise, to an executive position.

Betty snatched only two hours of disrupted sleep that night. She could not get to work fast enough the next morning to see her name posted on the board as one of the new officers. But when the promotion list was posted, Betty's name was not on it. She immediately went to her boss and said, "I don't understand what's going on." Her boss was equally puzzled and promptly confronted the CEO, who attempted to explain that Betty hadn't been an account executive long enough to be promoted. "What the hell has time got to do with the promotion?" Betty's boss demanded. Numerous excuses were made but none of them had anything to do with the fact that she was denied the pay raise and the promotion because she was female and Black. Betty's face and voice mirrored her pain and sorrow as she recalled:

> The reasons they gave for my not making the promotion list were getting fuzzier and fuzzier. Finally, one of the senior vice presidents told me, 'Well, you didn't make the list because you're not a team player.'
>
> 'I don't understand. What do you mean team player?' I asked.
>
> 'Well, Betty, you don't do a lot in terms of helping the other account executives in the department with some of their client relationships.'
>
> I said, 'That's not my job. I have my accounts and they have theirs. However, if someone would ask me for help, I would cooperate. No one could claim otherwise.'

Betty was very distraught because she had played the game by the letter and according to their rules. Even though they unexpectedly changed the rules on her several times, she managed to hurdle every obstacle.

After several days of officers huddling in the executive suites, Betty's boss came down to her office one afternoon and told her that omission of her name from the promotion list was an oversight. He assured her that her name would be on the next list, which was due in three months. When it was posted, Betty Dole was listed as a vice president. It was official: Betty became the first Black and first female vice president in the company's 75-year history.

Seven months after Betty's promotion, a Black just entering middle management filed a discrimination suit against the company. The chairman of the board, who was also the chief executive officer, summoned Betty to his office.

> 'Betty, I don't believe that we have ever discriminated against anybody,' he said. 'You know for a fact that you have been promoted faster than anyone who joined this company

at the same time that you did. Surely you cannot honestly say that you have been discriminated against.'

'Yes, I can,' Betty retorted.

'How can you say that?' he recoiled.

'Mr. Chairman, I can say it because of the changes I have had to go through in order to make vice president. With my training and ability, making vice president should have been a cake walk. If I had been a white male, the path to the vice presidency would have been laid out like a road map. But for me, a Black female, it wasn't—it was land mines and booby traps all the way. To this day, there are people in this company trying to set me up and steal my accounts, and I can name them.'

The chairman shook his head in disbelief and mumbled, 'I don't see it, Betty.'

Betty had every reason to believe that the chairman was speaking the truth because his daughter, with whom she had become friends, was employed by one of their competitors and faced the same discrimination as a female that Betty had encountered, without the added burden of racial discrimination.

Betty eventually accepted a position with another manufacturing company as a senior vice president, at a higher salary and more perks. Even today she is convinced that in his heart and soul, the chief executive officer of the corporation that made her a vice president never fully understood that he had ever discriminated against Blacks.

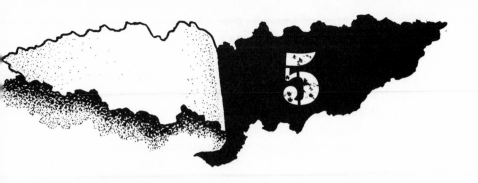

THE BLACK CIVIL SERVICE BOSS WHO WAS NOT PERMITTED TO TALK

Franz Hudson was born in Washington, D.C., May 7, 1940, and graduated from Paul Laurence Dunbar High School at the age of 16. Dunbar, at that time, was considered one of the best Black public secondary schools in the country because a large percentage of its graduates went on to college and successful careers.

For the first 65 years of this century, most career opportunities for bright young Black men like Franz Hudson were restricted to the ministry, civil service, education, or the railroad (where Pullman porters earned very little respect and received low wages but could hustle good tips). Franz' family was too poor to send him to college, but he was fortunate enough to obtain an internship with the Department of Agriculture, where he earned a scholarship to a college in the District.

Franz' civil service career began routinely, relative free of discrimination. But as he advanced in the system, racism jumped from its cocoon, besmirching everything from the water fountains to the soda fountains to transportation in D.C. Blacks could only ride in cabs that were owned and driven by other Blacks. Black-owned cabs weren't permitted to enter the horseshoe curve in front of the Union Train Station, an area reserved for the white-owned Yellow and Diamond taxis. Black women, men and children entering or leaving the nation's capital in the shadow of the White House were forced to carry their luggage for approximately a city block to find transportation.

Racism was so contagious in Washington that Black people were practicing it on one another. Circulars advertising single rooms for rent for "light colored folks only" were distributed on streetcars, which was the primary transportation for people of color. "When I was growing up, they used to say the reason that Blacks could not drive the streetcars or buses for the Capitol Transit Co. was because they couldn't count money or give the correct change," Hudson recalled. "Although it was not true, the establishment had many of us brainwashed into believing that kind of nonsense."

Blacks could not patronize or perform at any of the white theaters. When Gene Krupa's band appeared at the Lowe's Theater for a one-week engagement in January 1943, Black trumpet star Roy Eldridge received double pay for agreeing not to appear on stage or backstage with the band. Franz recalls the separate and unequal period of the 1940s and '50s when he stood in long lines outside of the Howard Theater, a "for colored" movie and live stage show house that featured such great Black stars as Duke Ellington, Cab Calloway, the Mills Brothers and Louis Armstrong.

Franz Hudson, though certainly a product of his environment, had not been so indoctrinated that he could not recognize that his intellect transcended stereotypes:

Although I knew that I was brighter than most of the white fellas that worked in my department, I had to be tested at every level, while watching whites receive their promotions without taking a test. They would move from grades 5 through 12 automatically, but not Franz Hudson. I was tested at every bloody step up the civil service ladder.

A white guy who started in the system at the same time I did frequently told me in advance when he was going to get a promotion. Then he would say, 'Franz, you are going to get a raise but you won't get yours for another five or six months.'

I used to question this fella about the unfairness, and he would simply shrug his shoulders and say, 'That's the system.' I was considered lucky because I was one of the acceptable Blacks awarded regular promotions, although never on time.

I did so well on my job that I was made acting supervisor over a crew of five or six white civil servants. My group was the best, but management refused to make me a permanent supervisor, although I knew and employed the standards better than anybody else in the department. They would not even consider a Black for that position, and gave it to a white guy who couldn't hold a candle for me on a dark night.

I was so angry that I confronted my superior. He said, 'Franz, I am sorry but the job you want is a white man's job. You know whites make more money than Blacks.' Then he ordered me to act as assistant to the new supervisor. Unfortunately, my new boss was so dense that he would not have recognized rain if it was blown in his face. They tried to soften the blow by telling me that if I would be patient, I'd get my turn.

I took my complaint to a Jewish fellow who was one of the senior supervisors in the department. He arranged without any rigamarole for my salary to be raised to a junior supervisor's level. But it really bothered me that the white guy got both the money and the title. I felt like Ted Lewis' shadow. (Ted Lewis, the orchestra leader, became famous in 1929 singing a song entitled, *Me and My Shadow*. His 'shadow' was Teddy Hale, a Black lad who danced behind Lewis, emulating every step in unison.)

The department heads wanted every office to run with the precision of a clock, but they didn't want me opening my mouth and bossing anybody. It was my duty to instruct and give directives to the supervisor daily, but never to the crew.

One day I finally got up enough nerve to go to the big boss, Harry Merriweather. He had a fine office with wood paneling and a huge oak desk with chairs to match. I told him that I wanted to be transferred out of the department and into the field, and reminded him that I had passed all the federal exams necessary to qualify.

Merriweather focused his steely blues straight into my brown eyes and said, 'You will never get that job in your lifetime.' What he was really saying was that no Blacks would ever work in the field.

Now, you've got to remember that he made that

statement in 1958, just three years after Dr. Martin Luther King Jr. led the Montgomery boycott. This was during the period that the People's Drug Store chain in the District of Columbia was still refusing to allow Blacks to sit at the regular lunch counters. Blacks were restricted to eating at a side counter reserved for colored people only. The bleak racial climate of the late 1950s spawned winds off of the Potomac River that whistled: "Segregation today, segregation tomorrow, segregation forever."

The winds of government began to shift in the latter part of the 1960s following the assassination of Dr. King. Exactly four months after King's death on April 4, 1968, Franz Hudson was called into Merriweather's office and given some good news. He had been appointed to the position of field representative in Detroit. Hudson was warned by his superior that he would find a lot of prejudice out there, and he did. The regional director of the Detroit office refused to speak to him, and let it be known that Hudson was not to be seen anywhere in the vicinity of the regional headquarters. Franz was provided with a small office several miles from the headquarters building in Paradise Valley, which was located in the heart of the Black community. He was further instructed to confine all of his activities to the Black neighborhoods.

Although Franz Hudson was quarantined, he was permitted to hire his own staff, and from time to time the regional director would send someone over to give him some directions and check on his progress. In spite of his isolation from the regional office, Franz developed a top-flight staff and performed so well that he eventually was offered a higher position in New York City.

The New York assignment was a page out of the same chapter of his earlier promotion, Hudson recalled:

When I arrived in New York, I was told by the regional director that I was the first Black to be assigned to that office. Then, he immediately dispatched me uptown to Harlem to open a branch that would service the Black and Hispanic communities.

After a relatively brief period, Hudson again rose above the ranks of the typical field supervisor because of his expertise in handling difficult assignments. Thus, he was summoned back to Washington, where he was informed that he had been promoted to regional director of the Los Angeles office, which was looked upon as the cesspool of the entire system.

Franz Hudson whipped that office into shape in about 18 months, prompting his superiors to assign a team from Washington to inspect the Los Angeles office.

Hudson was in a quandary. He tried without success to find out what type of inspection would be conducted. He even checked with other regional directors to see if they had ever undergone a similar visit from headquarters, but learned that such an inspection had not occurred before. The consensus was that the first Black regional director was being accorded special treatment.

Hudson recalled:

When the six inspectors arrived, they interviewed every white woman who worked in our office. The questions were centered around my interactions and relationships with the women, and whether we socialized or had any kind of personal after-hours relationship. The young women under my supervision had such respect for me that they told me the types of questions that were being asked of them by the inspectors.

After a week in our office, the inspection team rightly concluded that my relationships with the white magnolias was above reproach, by any standards. They returned to Washington with a smile on their faces, and wrote a glowing report commending me for being a credit to the colored race. (That is exactly the same statement that white America made when Jessie Owens won four gold medals in the 1936 Olympics held in Germany and when Joe Louis defeated James Braddock for the world heavyweight championship in Chicago in 1937.)

On another occasion, the national office sent out a team from the inspector general's office to audit my records. The audit was a response to the fact that I was the first regional director to ever award a $2 million contract to a Black-owned company. The award was legitimate in that the Black firm was the lowest bidder and the most qualified.

Hudson intuitively must have anticipated the audit because he never signed off on any of the bid contracts. This task was always performed by one of his capable white assistants. As a matter of fact, he let his assistant handle the entire contract bidding process. He simply orchestrated the work. Thus, after the auditors spent approximately one month going through every file page by page, they discovered that all the signatures on the contracts were those of white persons. This finding made them comfortable. Thus, Hudson became a good and trusted Black civil servant again. As a matter of fact, after the inspection was completed, Hudson called the other 11 regional directors and found out that none of them had ever been subjected to that type of audit. On the other hand, none of the other 11 regional managers had ever awarded a contract to a Black entrepreneur.

Grade 18 is the highest non-political rank a civil servant can be awarded within the bureau. Franz Hudson achieved that objective some years ago. However he still suffers intermittently from a burning sensation in the pit of his stomach caused by the Jim Crow treatment he encountered as he crawled up the civil service ladder.

Hudson had cultivated a stoic response to the pain of being on the receiving end of the whip of racial biasness. He chose not to get mad, but to get smart. His maneuvers were repaid in storybook manner: he subsequently became the boss of many of the white guys who had stepped on his fingernails as he clawed hand over hand out of a pit of mediocrity.

Hudson, the trouble shooter, received his umpteenth lateral promotion and was transferred back to Washington, where he was given the authority to change the behavior and public utterances of subordinates who dealt with minorities. Some employees who refused to change their means and ways either elected early retirement or changed bureaus.

Hudson's ultimate satisfaction arrived when he became the boss of the fellow who early in Hudson's career told him that another employee was more qualified for promotion because he was white and Hudson was Black. Franz worked hard and quietly to drum that fellow into early retirement.

PETER JOHNS: THE BLACK GIANT WHOSE LEGS WERE AMPUTATED AT THE KNEES BY CORPORATE AMERICA

Peter Johns was born in Philadelphia, Pa., May 11, 1939, a seventh child, and the only male in a family of 11 children. His father had managed to sandwich in a third-grade education among his share-cropping chores on Alex Ridoff's plantation in Lexington, Miss. The elder Johns migrated north in 1922 and found a job in a box factory in South Philadelphia, where he worked as a common laborer until he died in 1951. Johns never earned more than $50 a week during his lifetime.

Peter's mother was a grammar school graduate steeped in religious values and imbued with a strong Protestant work ethic, traits she apparently instilled in her children. Ten of the Johns offspring earned undergraduate degrees; two daughters are physicians, five are public schoolteachers and one is a professor of economics.

Young Johns, like his sisters, was an honors student in high school. He also was an accomplished musician on three instruments. Although he was offered a scholarship by the Juilliard School of Music in New York City, he had second thoughts about music as a career because he could not envision an opportunity during the 1950s for a Black oboe player in an all-white symphony orchestra. Thus, Johns applied to the Wharton School of Finance near his home. After graduating from

Wharton, he accepted a scholarship from the Massachusetts Institute of Technology at Cambridge, where he was awarded a master's and a doctorate in engineering.

In 1962, Peter embarked on a career in engineering. He signed on with the GYC Corporation, a company with an excellent in-service program that had a reputation as an upfront corporation with an equal opportunity commitment.

In reflecting on his early years at GYC, Peter Johns said:

My first assignment was working in the training program at the GYC plant in Syracuse, N.Y. In 1965, when we graduated from that program, Henry Ruggles, one of my classmates, was offered a position with GYC's operation in Daytona Beach, Fla. Henry eagerly accepted, and couldn't understand my reluctance to join him.

He'd been there only a few weeks when he called me and said, 'Peter, you gotta come down.' I told him I didn't want to come down there and get humiliated and stepped on every day. He said, 'Don't worry. I can assure you that everything will be okay.'

When I got off the plane at Daytona Beach, I was met by Henry, his wife Kathy and their 2-year-old kid. Hans, their little boy, was running through my legs playing a phantom version of ring around the roses while we waited for my luggage. The kid and my right leg drew a lot of attention from white folks in the terminal. The kid's merriment with my leg so distracted one white fellow that he walked into a plate-glass window.

When they dropped me at the hotel in downtown Daytona Beach, there were about 25 people lined up to register. Henry had pre-registered me, but I could only watch as other travelers were registered and ushered to their rooms in very short order. I made several trips to the registration desk to see if they had forgotten me. The assistant manager began to sound like a parrot: 'No, we're getting your room ready. Just be patient.'

After about an hour, an old Black gentleman in janitorial garb shuffled up to me and said, 'I will take your bags.' I later learned from the elderly suitcase toter that the white bellboys had an unwritten policy of not putting their hands on luggage that belonged to 'colored people.'

As I followed the old gent out of the front door into the moonless night, I asked, 'Where are we going?'

'We are going to put you up in a deluxe cottage on the beach,' he replied. We walked for what seemed like a Philadelphia city block before we reached the cottage.

The next morning, I awakened to swishing sounds, which turned out to be from the waves of the Atlantic Ocean along the beach. During a brief walking survey, I discovered that I was the only person assigned to a cottage on that beach. August was an off-season month for the hotel, and it was hard to find transportation. To make bad matters worse, cabs would not pick up Black passengers. The hotel manager finally arranged to get a black-owned jitney to carry me out to the GYC plant.

When I arrived at the company, I told my white friends that there was no way in the world that I would be able to stay in that town. GYC had a fair housing policy, but it was obvious that it had never been tested. I left Daytona Beach after two days and took a position with the company in Philadelphia.

The housing experience was repeated, with some modifications, wherever I was assigned: in King of Prussia, a suburb of Philadelphia, and in Santa Barbara, Calif.

Erie, Pa., was the pits. There was hardly a place for a Black person to eat in that town except McDonald's and a couple of greasy spoons.

Erie was the only city where clubs really became important because there weren't many public restaurants. The better dining places were private clubs such as the Polish Sharpshooter's Club and the Italian American Club. Because I was Black, I was automatically excluded from membership in those organizations.

Although I was the highest-ranking Black at GYC in Erie, and we were the only Blacks living on executive row, I was never invited to membership in the country club. Everyone else on executive row who worked for GYC belonged to some country club, but not Peter Johns.

Erie was a tough town, a blue-collar, red-neck town and a terrible place for a Black to live. Psychologically, it got to me faster than any other city we were ever housed in. I finally told my wife one day, 'I've gotta leave this place. GYC is a nice place to work. They are polite, but I've gotta leave. I cannot take this environment any longer.'

I decided if you are a Black man in America, you've certainly got to attempt to adjust to the fact that you are a third-class citizen. And I learned early that if you let every racist slight get to your head, you'd be enraged most of your waking hours and your nerves would become so tender that you could become a prime candidate for a heart attack before you reached your 40th birthday. It's my opinion that one way to avoid such a premature tragedy is to work on the premise that you can only fight on one battle front at a time. I decided that belonging to a country club would not be the turf over which I would have a stroke.

My agenda was to make a serious contribution to the corporate world. I would show people that I could get to the top.

I thought the fastest track to success would be the business side of the corporate ladder rather than the social side. However, I recognize that there is no way in the world that a Black man can succeed in corporate America without running into some good intentioned white folks. I knew there was no pathway to the top of the heap without some help.

One day a white colleague who was nearing the age of retirement said to me, 'You are a hardworking young man. You are a bright boy. You seem to have all the requirements to make it with this company. I hope you won't get angry with me for giving you some unsolicited advice.

First of all, you're going to have to work twice as hard as your white counterparts. I don't care what you think. You're gonna have to work twice as hard because you are a Black man. It is unfair but it is a fact of life. You are also gonna have to be morally straight (meaning don't fool around with white women.) If you will accept those axioms, I will help you as much as I can.'

As I look back over my career, I found that that old gentleman was one of three white individuals who gave me a hand as I moved up the corporate ladder. Plus, I was an

oddity because during the mid '60s, when there were few
Blacks trying to rise in a Fortune 500 company on the fast
track, I was attractive to the corporate fathers because my
whole being radiated confidence. My confidence was not a
facade: I am competent, Black and personable. The only
possible derailment that could fall across my track was
confrontation.

Peter believed that to win the battles for promotions in corporate
America, you have to minimize your enemies list by skirting confrontation when and wherever possible. You plan your strategy like an army
general: you don't leak your plan until after you have made your move.
Employing that tactic, you avoid being ambushed on the way up the
corporate ladder. Competition that is forewarned will make every
effort to round up a posse and cut you off at the pass.

It was Peter Johns' opinion that publicity created jealousy and
animosity, and when he broke loose from the herd and started rising
toward the top of the corporate ladder, he made every effort to avoid
media contact. Peter wouldn't even permit his picture to be taken for
the company newsletter or the local newspapers because he didn't
want it to be generally known that there was a Black man on the move.

The chief executive officer of the parent company desperately
needed somebody to put between himself and a subsidiary corporate
structure that had an inordinate appetite for debt. Thus, he decided as a
last resort to make a talented Black man the scapegoat.

When Johns finally was offered the presidency he hesitated before
accepting. He knew that several whites, who were less capable, had
been approached but had refused to captain the sinking ship. But Johns
also was astute enough to recognize that for most people, Black or
white, opportunity seldom knocks twice. For Johns, one knock was
enough. He was knowledgeable about the holes in the bowels of the
partially submerged ship and he knew exactly what needed to be
jettison to keep the corporate boat afloat.

Unlike another Black scapegoat, Samuel Pierce, former secretary
of the U.S. Department of Housing and Urban Development (HUD),
Johns was a hands-on chief operating officer who was able to stop the
corporate ship from listing and thereby change its course. The paradox
is that the CEO who appointed Johns as a scapegoat subsequently
received accolades, not only for turning the failing subsidiary company
into a profit center, but for having the foresight to appoint a Black man

to stand watch at the helm.

As president and COO of the subsidiary, Johns traveled in circles with others of the same rank, who tended to forget that he was Black. Some of those who caught themselves making stereotypical remarks about Blacks in Johns' presence apologized for their slip of the lip.

Once, when the company was looking for a chief financial officer, a member of the search committee, while in Johns' presence, remarked, "Well, there's no way that we can consider a Black person for this position because they cannot understand the complexities of finance. Even if we hired one, there's no way in the world he would stay on the job."

At this point, Peter Johns intervened: "What am I and what do you mean?" The non-verbal response was reflected in a bunch of beet-red faces around the conference table. Johns observed:

> Most whites have been trained to think of Blacks in a stereotypical fashion. If they're around a Black of equal or superior intelligence, they tend to forget momentarily that he's Black, even though they interface with him daily. They never really change their views, they just simply make the peer Black an honorary white. They include you in the conversation when there's a need for a Black point of view, but they do not consider you as an integral part of their intellectual fellowship.

The chances of a Black man becoming the CEO of a Fortune 500 corporation without being a part of the old boys' network are slim to none unless a company is financially controlled by a chairman who is committed to promoting minorities on merit. The run-of-the-mill corporate board is one of the last bastions of the white power structure.

The zenith of Peter Johns' career arrived the day he thought he had broken through the white power structure. He entertained this notion because his white mentor confided that he wanted Johns to succeed him as CEO when he stepped down the following year. Johns felt that he had become the chosen one because of his performance in turning the subsidiary company around while operating strictly by the corporate rules. Those may have been the original reasons for the retiring CEO's commitment, but the giant whose legs were amputated at the knees made one mistake. He violated his own rule and permitted his picture to appear on the front page of a prestigious national magazine along with a feature story that gave a detailed description of the changing of the guards and Johns' impending coronation.

When Johns' former mentor first saw the picture it was during a flight on company business, when a flight attendant handed him a copy of the magazine. If the CEO's rage could have been converted into jet power, the plane would have ascended another 30,000 feet.

Johns' mentor suddenly turned into a tormentor and began to make things difficult for Johns at every turn. Peter became terribly perplexed and confided in Malcolm Durham, a white friend who served on several boards with him. "You're dead," said Malcolm, an executive headhunter. "This is typical. Do you know how many times the first heir apparent succeeds the CEO?"

Malcolm showed Peter a study that indicated that only 11 percent of the initial heirs are actually crowned, and that the mantle usually falls on the shoulders of the third person under consideration. By the third time around, Malcolm said, the board of directors and the search committee have reached the point of no return with a lame duck CEO who turns from mentor to monster when confronted by his successor.

Peter Johns crossed the line of no return when he challenged the CEO to keep his commitment or to fire him. The CEO did neither. He simply kept Johns twisting slowly in a wind that carried a –50 degree wind chill factor. Although Peter's wolf-ticket tactics failed, he expected to at least make a lateral move to another Fortune 500 company. Unfortunately, it wasn't to be. The market was not looking for a talented Black man who would accept only a top position with a prestigious corporation.

Peter Johns was on a first-name basis with some of the officers at the Boston Consulting Group, an international consulting firm. One of his friends, when told of Johns' predicament, was optimistic. "Peter, your phone is going to ring off the hook."

The consultant, a longtime partner with the Boston company, based his assurance on the need for outstanding executives in many corporations around the country.

Peter Johns was more realistic. His encounters with the sword of prejudice throughout his career left him skeptical of receiving unbiased consideration for the No. 1 or No. 2 positions.

Peter, although proud of his talents and experience, knew his phone would not "ring off the hook." And it hasn't. After almost two years and some 40 recommendations from the headhunters, Peter has received only one serious offer for an interview with a Fortune 500 company.

The bottom line in American corporate policy, particularly if you are Black, is: Never outshine the person who writes the check unless you are willing to risk becoming an amputee.

AUTHOR'S NOTE

In July 1989, Peter Johns affiliated with KBA Limited Partnership, a venture capital firm in New Jersey. In January 1990, Johns and two partners successfully bid for Monotype Corporation T.L.C. in Surrey, England. Peter Johns is the president (or managing director, as the position is called in the United Kingdom,) of the holding company.

Johns believes that the acquisition of Monotype, a high-tech electronic publishing company, is the first step toward creating a global empire.

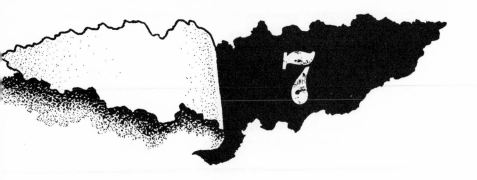

"THEY WANTED WHITE BREAD AND I WAS WHOLE WHEAT"

Frank Smith Jr., was the third of four children born to Frank and Lucille Smith. His debut on March 3, 1950, was a happy day for the family: Frank Sr. declared his son would be a doctor.

The elder Smith, a veteran of World War II, felt he would have been a physician if his education had not been interrupted in March 1942 when his local draft board called him to serve in the U.S. Army. Frank Sr. found work as a mail carrier after his discharge from the army in September 1945, and Frank Jr. was born five years later.

A stethoscope, doctor's bag and candy pills were among the gifts Frank Jr. received on his third birthday. Sending a child through college and medical school was a gigantic dream for Frank's parents since Frank Sr., up until 1950, had never earned more than $1.40 per hour working as a civil servant. To make a bad matter worse, Frank Sr. was a male chauvinist who subscribed to the "keep them barefoot and pregnant" theory and insisted that his wife stay home and take care of their children.

When Frank reached the age of five, he was enrolled in the University of Chicago Lab School at a great financial sacrifice to the family. The $2,000-per-year tuition represented 40 percent of Frank Sr.'s annual income, but no price was too high for preparing their son to become a physician. Young Frank received better-than-average grades at the Lab School, although his teachers reported that he was not performing up to his capabilities. Schoolwork was no challenge to him, so the bored young man engaged in childish pranks that disrupted other members of his class. His mother Lucille spent a great deal of time meeting with the principal and defending her child's behavior before it was discovered that Frank Jr.'s behavioral problem was a byproduct of a high energy level and a severe case of egoism. The Smiths had transmitted to their son their firm conviction that Frank was smarter than anyone else in his school.

Young Frank's behavioral problem was resolved in part when the principal assigned him to extra gym classes where he siphoned off some of his excess energy. He learned to love both track and basketball, but was not very good at either sport. His athletic deficiency humbled and humanized the bright young man into recognizing that becoming a total person meant more than academic achievements.

Frank Jr. was awarded a scholarship to Northwestern University in Evanston, Ill., in 1967. Affirmative action was on the march when Frank entered Northwestern, which had a number of supportive programs for non-white undergraduates. A dean for minority students helped to keep them on track and serve as a resource for students who needed assistance with their studies. By the time Frank Jr. reached his senior year, his academic performance was on par with the national average of students competing for medical school.

The four years Frank spent at Northwestern proved to be the golden years for middle class Blacks chasing the academic rainbow. Doors opened by President Lyndon Baines Johnson's push for civil rights legislation slammed shut after President Richard Milhouse Nixon's initial thrust for Black capitalism between 1969 and 1971. The federal programs that had aided Black economic and academic progress for the decade between 1965 and 1975 had died by 1990, or are bedded down in intensive care and fed intravenously by a life-support system interconnected with patched tubing.

In 1971, several months before Frank graduated from Northwestern University, he was stricken with a severe case of minority paranoia. Frank was deathly afraid that he would not gain acceptance by an accredited medical school in the United States although he had applied to approximately 25 medical institutions and paid roughly $500 in application fees. The fees were not spent in vain because when the responses began rolling in, Frank was delighted to find only six rejections and 19 acceptances. The choice of schools became easy when the University of Illinois Medical School in Chicago offered him a full four-year scholarship. Frank said:

> Medical school is a whole different ballgame. The talent level is 5 times that in college, and the competitiveness is 10 times as focused. Instead of 4,000 or 40,000 students, the faculty is dealt 100 to 150 students, and could more easily assess each individual. On balance, the professors treated you fairly. I saw no evidence of blatant racism on the part of the professional staff people.
>
> However, the whites had their own study groups when I was in med school, and the Blacks gravitated together for survival. Only two of the four Blacks in my group graduated on schedule. One graduated a year late, and the other fellow never got past his second year.
>
> As I said before, there was no *overt* racism. It was silent. In the classroom you got the basic minimum and nothing more. There was little to no small talk after class between the Black students and professors.
>
> To fill the academic gap, a few of the former graduates of the Medical Center developed a minority teaching program and they came back regularly to help those Black students who needed some assistance. The grads passed along old exams and taught review courses prior to exams because the minority med students had no way of tapping into the white boys' network. White students generally don't share old exams with their Black classmates.
>
> During my first year in med school, I was a loner who did not recognize the need for a Black network. I caught academic hell. The professors were dumping out huge volumes of work daily. I found it hard if not impossible to digest and understand all of that material in such a relatively short period of time. I spent 8½ hours a day listening to lectures. The end product is that I had difficulty passing my first-year examinations.
>
> I discovered that many of the students found it to their advantage to teach themselves out of the textbooks at their own tempos. Instead of wasting time in lectures, they got their material straight from the printed page. And I learned

that transcriptions of the entire lectures were available. Nobody told me during my freshman year that fewer than 50 percent of the med students nationwide attended the daily lectures. That kind of information was picked up in white fraternities and Black networks. A high percentage of Black students flunk out of medical schools early in the game because there's no Black buddy system.

I discovered late in my fourth year of medical school that overt racism wasn't dead at the University of Illinois. It was simply hiding in the wings. I asked the dean of students to write me a letter of recommendation that would aid me in getting accepted in a hospital residential program. The dean of students performed that service in June of every year for qualified graduates. The letter usually summed up the grad's academic history at the school in a manner that promoted his candidacy for residency in a teaching hospital.

When I received my letter, I almost went into shock. There was no mention of my capabilities or my personality. The 10-line impersonal letter said absolutely nothing about my medical and academic skills.

I had seen some of the letters the dean had written for the white students. They were filled with glittering recommendations that spilled over into two—and sometimes three—pages. When I complained to the dean that the letter she wrote for me was inadequate, she offered to rewrite it. I did not accept her offer because I did not feel that I could trust her.

Instead, I asked the Black dean of minority affairs to write a letter on my behalf. He responded with a recommendation that reflected my performance during the four years I spent in medical school.

My first choice was to take my residency in orthopedics, my second choice was general surgery and my third choice was obstetrics and gynecology.

My first round of letters resulted in only one response: Howard University. They said they had a waiting list of four orthopedic candidates. Two of them were Howard graduates that they were committed to accept in their program. I thought that meant my chances were almost nil, however, I was determined to hold out another year for an orthopedics match.

It is very difficult for a Black or white doctor who did not score in the top 10 percent of the class to be placed in orthopedics or surgery. That is, unless one has a parent who was a doctor or someone in the family who socialized with the chairman of the department. In some instances, knowing a member of a hospital board who also happens to be a heavy contributor to the hospital might be a passport to a residency. I did not have any contacts, except the lens in my eyes. My option was to pray.

Suddenly, I had a stroke of luck. A local hospital offered me a one-year program. Unfortunately, there were no other Black doctors at this hospital, no colleagues for me to huddle with. My tour of duty in the department of general surgery was a cappella.

I hadn't been in the department too long before I sensed that they were trying to remake me into another image, one that was acceptable to them. If I expressed my personality in any way, I was viewed as cocky, a talented person who needed to be fenced in.

I was told not to reveal emotions in my voice. I was not to show any affection to any of my favorite patients who came into my office. If I had a smile on my face, I was ordered to erase it. This Negro is too happy, they said. Oh, no! I was too cavalier. Yes, that's the word. I was too cavalier. They wanted white bread and I was whole wheat.

Although a gregarious person, I was not invited to any social events at the hospital or to dinner parties given by the senior physicians with whom I worked daily. I would have been delighted to have been included in some of these affairs, but that was not to be.

There is an effort, in my opinion, to isolate and discredit Black men in medicine. It revolves around shifting the blame. In the medical field, when something bad happens, things tend to filter downhill. Since Black guys are usually at the bottom of the hill, the blame falls on them.

Once I was called to assist in an operation 20 minutes before the surgery was to take place. Ordinarily I would have had an opportunity to meet the patient and review the medical history before such a procedure. In this situation, I was told to scrub for 10 minutes, which is routine, before joining the attending physician. We both gowned, gloved up and commenced the operation. It was a hernia repair on the left side.

About 20 minutes into the operation, the nurse said, 'Dr. X, the consent statement says right hernia repair.' I nearly had an accident in my pants when I realized we were operating on the wrong side.

I was devastated. I had visions of being fired, of being banned from medicine for life. At this point, I wasn't the most popular person in the hospital anyway, so I was very concerned.

Five minutes after the mistake was discovered, chills and sweat enveloped my body. I passed out and I was told that my head hit the floor like a rock. They called a code on me. A code is employed when additional medical personnel are needed to assist somebody who has usually had a near-fatal occurrence, like a heart attack.

When I regained consciousness, I went to my room and started packing my belongings because I knew I was fired. Before I could finish packing, I was called into the office and given a reprieve by the director after I gave him a detailed description of the events leading up to the operation and the operation itself. He said that since I was assisting, the responsibility went to the surgeon in charge. He also reminded me that a full-fledged doctor can't blame a medical student or a resident who assists him for the doctor's own mistake.

The hernia case developed into a lawsuit, and, believe it or not, the doctor actually tried to blame me for his mistake.

When you get involved in a situation like this where Black and white are concerned, you're gonna wonder how much of this is racism and how much of this is just business. Of course, they usually say it's all business but I'm gonna say it's 90 percent racism because that is the nature of the animal.

In spite of the operating room debacle, I completed the local hospital program without a blemish on my record.

When I applied for an orthopedics residency the second time, I was really certain that I was gonna get it. When it failed to come through, I had no back-up plan. I had to resort to the use of a medical hotline and newsletters to find out about the jobs that were available across the country.

I had mentally jettisoned any thoughts of pursuing orthopedics for a third time. I also decided to skip surgery and go for my third option, obstetrics and gynecology. This brought me to Boston, where I was fortunate to get into an excellent OB-GYN training program.

I was hired directly by the chairman of the department. I think he brought me aboard without any bias to my race, but the hospital was certainly short of Black people. I was the only Black doctor. I started out at ground zero.

My boss and the other doctors at the hospital were Italians. I learned to laugh at Italian jokes and was introduced to Italian food. I had never eaten tortellini, which was a surprise to them. They even taught me how to pick out good Italian wines.

My boss was a Catholic and he expected me to learn the history of his church. As we made the hospital rounds, Dr. S. would talk about the lives of the saints, and stare at me as though I were some devil worshipper because I had not heard about them before. All of my religious experience has been in the Presbyterian Church, so how was I supposed to know about Catholicism? On the other hand, I'd bet my life that Dr. S. knew absolutely nothing about Malcolm X except that he's supposed to hate him.

The doctors attempted to make me feel like Captain Dumbo because I didn't understand their culture. They frequently would speak Italian exclusively whenever I was around, which, in my opinion, was impolite. I did not know what the heck they were talking about. They could be calling me nigger to my face and at the same time laughing and shaking my hand.

Residents nationwide are given an annual in-service examination. The first time I took it I ranked in the 75th percentile. The doctors were so pleased that they started calling me 'Sonny boy.' After that test, they never called me by name. They'd say, 'Hey, Sonny boy,' or 'Here comes Sonny boy.' I wanted to tell my boss that I did not enjoy joking and I would have been pleased if I never heard the nickname of 'Sonny boy' again in my life.

But whenever he called me 'Sonny boy,' I'd smile. I don't know why. It was probably an instinctive effort to survive. When two Black female residents became members of the department, they were called, 'the girls.'

It's funny because this 'Sonny boy' moniker could go both ways. When my supervisor was happy to see me, he'd call out, 'Here's my Sonny boy.' But he could inject sarcasm in that nickname in a way you wouldn't believe. I often wondered if he wanted me to fall down on one knee and give him an imitation of Al Jolson's corkface rendition of *Sonny Boy* or *Swanee*.

So I continued to smile and score in the 75th percentile through my first three years in the residency. In my fourth year, I kicked butt by scoring in the 90th percentile of the test takers. Their general reaction to me changed once more. I remember one of my professors asking the class how we had done that year on the in-service examination. Some students said they'd scored in the 60th percentile, others scored in the 70s. He asked who got the highest score. After what seemed like 30 seconds of silence, someone said, 'Frank.'

'Frank who?' he asked. Keep in mind this guy had been teaching me for three years. The fellows pointed at me and the doctor said, 'Him?' I was personally offended by his response but I couldn't dare show it. I was still 'Sonny boy,' but with a negative tint.

I was rewarded for making the highest score by being appointed the chief resident. I now suspect that they were after my ass for no other reason than they probably perceived me a lot differently than they had before.

It was as though my superiors started looking into the depths of my eyes, trying to see what made me tick and what my motivations and goals were. They just didn't like me all of sudden because I had excelled beyond 'white bread.' It was like they wanted to stick their feet out in front of me to see if I would trip.

In obstetrics and gynecology, you can easily trip because there are many crises that demand immediate medical response. The person in charge is the chief resident, the most senior doctor. Dr. Frank Smith witnessed first-hand how the white chief residents manipulated the nursing staff in emergency situations. Sometimes they used strong language like, 'Move your ass. I want this now,' or 'I want your butt over here.'

Dr. Smith made these observations six weeks after he became the chief resident:

> In the OB-GYN department, tension was usually high. Friction was high. Nurses who had been my friends changed when I became chief. Suddenly I was Mr. Asshole, although I was the same person they laughed, talked and had drinks with for more than three years. They viewed me through different eyes because this Black boy was in charge. They had to do what I said.
>
> The nurses got very upset and, without my knowledge, met with the administration to describe the unpleasant environment they said had taken over the department. A Black cloud was hanging over the delivery room at this point. To my astonishment, I was even accused of fondling one of the nurses. The accusation resulted in an administrative hearing that adjourned without charges because the accuser refused to step forward.

Racist treatment against the Black doctor was not the private preserve of the professional staff. The patients also got their licks in.

> I recall a case where the white doctor who was in charge of the case was outside of the hospital having lunch. His patient went into labor faster than expected. The baby was positioned to arrive any minute. The nurses had put the expectant mother in the delivery suite and had propped her legs up in the stirrups. I scrubbed and gowned, gloved and walked into the room. I finished preparing the patient and was standing at her feet while her husband was sitting at the head of the table on her right side. He looked up at me with his blue eyes and asked as clear as day, 'Are you the doctor?'
>
> I just felt a negative energy swell up inside of me. I knew exactly what he meant: 'You couldn't be the doctor. There must be somebody else that's going to come into this

room and save my little white angel.'

I chilled, swallowed my pride, and said, 'Yes, I am the doctor,' and proceeded to deliver the baby.

Mistaken identity is a common experience Black doctors frequently endure. When we walk into a patient's room, we often don't get the respect automatically accorded to a white physician. The expectation level drops the moment we appear. The last thing that most white people expect to see is a Black doctor walking in a room.

One day when I was an intern, I walked into a wealthy patient's private room with my glasses on, dressed in my neatly pressed white laboratory coat, a stethoscope in my pocket and a clipboard in my hand—all the trappings of the medical profession. The patient said, 'You must be here for the garbage.'

Without giving her a chance to say anymore, I said, 'Yes, you!' Then she really looked at me and quickly changed her tune. 'Don't get me wrong. I didn't mean it the way it sounded. I didn't mean anything personal.

'Neither did I,' I said and left.

Black doctors often are mistaken for the TV man, a cafeteria worker, an orderly or nurse, but rarely for a physician.

Even when I was the chief resident, some of my peers tried to stick their feet out in my path so they could make me fall.

In one instance, a mother had died during surgery. They tried to say that the young woman's death was a case of medical mismanagement. I was not in the hospital at the time nor was I scheduled to be but someone even went so far as to say that I shouldn't have allowed the baby to born.

The question is how do you stop a natural progression of events that are beyond your control? In this case, I was backed up by the obstetrics and gynecology department, and our internal review committee, composed of physicians from other departments. I was completely cleared of the charges.

Yet, within a month after the death of that young mother, I was transferred, without explanation, to a hospital with a large Black patient population.

It was evident that for my white colleagues, one thin slice of whole wheat bread was too much. They wanted a whole loaf of white bread, and they got it.

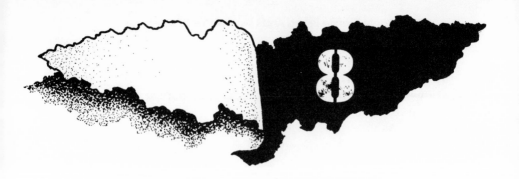

THE U.S. ARMY TAUGHT GARY FORTUNĒ WHAT IT MEANT TO BE BLACK

Gary Fortunē was born in Milwaukee, Wisc., October 10, 1925., the oldest of three children born to a union between Donald and Rosemarie. Gary's parents were natives of New Orleans. His father Donald was the first born in a family of 10, which included three sisters and six brothers, and his mother Rosemarie was the second youngest among nine siblings.

In 1916, a year before the United States entered World War I, Donald and Rosemarie migrated to Milwaukee via Tampa, Fla., New York City and Montreal, Canada. They were in search of a market for their hand-rolled cigars. The popular and expensive handmade private brands were being drastically underpriced by the John Ruskin, White Owl and other manufactured cigars. Within eight months after Donald and Rosemarie settled in their adopted hometown, Donald's nine brothers and sisters followed them to the industrial north, where they secured work in cigar factories and made their own brand of hand-rolled cigars in their homes for neighbors and friends.

It was very easy for the light-skinned Fortunēs to cross the color line and pass for white in Milwaukee, a city that was a heavy influx of dark-skinned ethnic groups. With the exception of Donald and two of his brothers, the Fortunēs married white folks, and secured employment under the guise of being white.

Gary resembled his father although Gary's complexion was some-times described as a "East Indian tan," whereas, Donald was a pure "French white." The Fortunēs lived in an all-white neighborhood and the family wanted Gary to be anything but colored. Based on the occasion, Gary could easily pass himself off as a Hawaiian, East Indian, Greek, Syrian or Sicilian. The Fortunē children were not permitted to socialize with Blacks. Young Fortunē was culturally white and proud of it.

After Gary and his two sisters reached their teens, their mother put them in touch with reality by introducing them to Chicago's Black middle class society through her sister, who resided in Bronzeville (Chicago's Harlem). All of their social discourse with Blacks was on the South Side of Chicago during weekends. The kids had no social life in Milwaukee outside of school.

Because of his mother's protective maneuvers, Gary was shielded from cultural shock until he joined the Army during World War II. He and many of his University of Wisconsin classmates went down to the draft board together to enlist in the service and all but Gary were shipped off to Camp Grant, Ill. Gary was ordered to report to the 1609th Negro induction center at Camp Custer in Battlecreek, Mich. It was in Camp Custer that he was figuratively thrown into a cold shower with all kinds of Black folks. Gary recalls:

I was dumb. I was green. I didn't understand their language. I was in deep, deep trouble. It was a very interesting experience and kind of humbling. I knew nothing about Black history. I had never heard of Nat Turner, Phyllis Wheatley, Harriet Tubman, Dr. W.E.B. DuBois or Frederick Douglass. The longer I stayed in the Army the more I realized how little I knew about my own people. I even asked a fellow in our barracks where he got the name of Booker.

He said, 'Booker T. Washington.'

'Who's that?' I asked. I didn't know that Booker T. Washington was the great educator who founded the Tuskegee Institute in Tuskegee, Ala. There had been nothing in my experience in Wisconsin that indicated to me that knowing any of these things was important. This whole business of not knowing within my gut that I was Black, but recognizing it intellectually, was a painful conflict.

I was finally jarred into the total realization that I was Black because I was treated like one. For example, the Army sent me to Augusta, Ga., to attend a special training program. I had read that Augusta had been the playground of Gen. (Dwight D.) Eisenhower, who used to golf down there.

After retreat I would head to town and go out with a young lady who became kind of special to me. This girl looked like she was white, but she was Black. I picked her up late one afternoon to take a bus ride and we headed for the back of the bus where Black folks were supposed to be. There was only one vacant seat in the back of the bus and she took that. I stood, hanging on a strap. Because I wanted to see the city that General Eisenhower called the 'garden spot of America,' I leaned over to look out of the window. I was absorbed in the landscape and beautiful homes when some white guy tapped me on the shoulder and said, 'We don't allow niggers to hang over white women down here.'

I snapped, 'Ain't no white woman sitting in that seat. She's Black.' I was an innocent babe in the woods. It's a wonder that I got out of Georgia alive!

Washington, D.C., was no better than Georgia or Mississippi. The whole notion of being considered part of the military was just devastating to me. I was wearing this goddamn uniform and I couldn't even go into a restaurant. There were times when we Blacks had to get off the sidewalk and walk in the streets to make room for white people to walk together on the sidewalk. The only theaters we could go to in Washington were the Howard, the Lincoln and the Booker T. There were a couple of nightclubs, like the Crystal Cavern, where we could go, but all of the other places were off limits.

I will never forget when I was on maneuvers in Louisiana. We had been out for several weeks and ended up without food for two days. We stopped at a little hole-in-the-wall restaurant to eat and they made us all go to the back door, where they gave us all some chow in greasy doggie bags. For me the U.S. Army was a real awakening of what it was like to be Black in America. To me it was a totally foreign experience because there was nothing in my childhood or young adulthood that had prepared me for what I ran into head-on within the military service.

After Fortunē was discharged from the Army in 1946, he returned to Madison to finish the requirements for his degree in aeronautical engineering at the University of Wisconsin. In the interim, he married. Gary believed that the degree would be his passport to decent employment. Fortunē and 2,000 other graduates walked across the stage and received their sheepskins in June 1949.

There were only two other Blacks in the 1949 graduation class. One of them, Peter Lash, was a very handsome fair-skinned man who seemed to disappear into thin air after receiving his degree. None of his classmates has heard from or seen him since graduation day. Fortunē and the other Black grad assume that Peter is somewhere passing for white.

Fortunē managed to obtain only one interview before he graduated. During the interview, Gary revealed that he would like to go into marketing. The interviewer responded that he didn't think Gary had a snowball's chance in hell of getting into marketing with his or any other company. "Are you saying I have just wasted four years going to school? What are you telling me?" Gary demanded.

"I don't want to put it that way. But I just don't think you will find any work in marketing," the recruiter replied.

Nineteen forty-nine was a bad year economically, and white folks caught colds. That being the case, Black folks caught pneumonia. Fortunē pounded the streets of several Midwestern cities in search of employment. The G.I. Bill helped him keep his skin and bones together by joining the "52/20 club," which was created by congressional legislation passed in 1944 and provided for World War II veterans to collect $20 a week for 52 weeks while they were going through an adjustment period and searching for employment.

By November 1949, Gary had given some thought to working for a shoe store where he had been employed during his high school years. But his wife warned him, "If you do that, you will never get out of that shoe store," and he followed her advice.

Gary finally found a job as a mail carrier. One of his postal supervisors found out he had a engineering degree and advised him to "Get the hell out of here, because there is no place for you to go but to hell in the post office."

About a year after he began working for the post office, Fortunē was recommended by a friend for a job at a small manufacturing company that built bombing navigation computers for B-52 bombers. He indicates that it was an interesting job although it required no engineering skills. The guys who sat next to him were high school graduates who performed the same kind of work at higher wages simply because they were white.

Gary Fortunē had been underemployed for five years before he had an opportunity to utilize his university background. In the spring of 1954, Gary got a lead from his brother-in-law, who said there was an opening in the plant where he worked in Newark, N.J. Fortunē leaped at the opportunity, and became the first Black graduate hired by the WVAN Corporation as an engineer.

Fortunē had worked at the plant for just two months when it finally dawned on him that only two of the more than 100 co-workers in his department really accepted him. Many simply rejected him on face value, because it was Black.

Gary learned about many of these criticisms from his supervisor during his first performance review. The supervisor told Gary that he couldn't find anything wrong with his work, but most of his colleagues had registered strong objections to his presence. Some didn't like the cologne he used, and others claimed to be distracted by Gary's whistling, a habit he acquired from his father, who always whistled while he worked around the house. Fortunē suspected that the hidden reason behind his co-workers' objections was the overly friendly attitude several beautiful young white women displayed toward him in the office. Although the handsome Fortunē was not the playboy type, he was viewed as a definite threat by most white men.

One person who had Fortunē on his short hate list was his performance appraiser, who intimated that Gary was a slow learner, and intimated that he didn't see any future for him at the company. Of course this was all contrived nonsense.

In the face of all the negativism surrounding him on the job, Fortunē was pleasantly surprised to find a salary increase when he received his next check:

> I got my check and said, 'Gee, this looks wrong.' I was kind of reluctant to cash it, but in my economic circumstances I couldn't afford not to cash it. After receiving the third check for the increased amount, I still thought it was a mistake. I

called the payroll department and said, 'I really wish you
guys would get squared away with my check. I wish you
could check and see if you have made a mistake.' They got
back to me in a relatively short period and said, 'Oh, you got
a raise. Didn't anybody tell you?'

'No, nobody had told me.'

The department supervisor had raised my salary over
the objection of the performance appraiser, and the raise set
up an iron wall of resentment between me and the
appraiser. The pissed-off appraiser had not bothered to tell
me that I had gotten a raise.

In early 1960, when I was promoted to crew supervisor,
I was required to go on various locations with a crew. I later
learned that certain crew members actually drew lots to
determine who was gonna ride with me. One of the guys in
the group said, 'Oh hell, he smells all right. And he eats his
noon meal out of a lunch box the same as we do.' Keep in
mind this is a group of white funky blue-collar workers
making an assessment of their white-collar Black boss.

An announcement by the top brass that Gary was promoted to
head up one of the engineering departments shocked many of the
white engineers, but he soon gained their respect through his knowledge of the work and administrative skills. Fortunē, who had a hands-
on management style, recalls:

When I worked in engineering, I wasn't working as a Black
person or dealing only with Black problems. I was dealing
with all of the problems. At that time some of the largest
customers in our system were my responsibility. I was able
to do things as an engineer in those days that young
engineers—Black or white—couldn't do today. The speed of
communication and the computer and centralization have
made the kind of autonomy that I enjoyed impossible.

Gary Fortunē was really on the move when the president of the
company promoted him to vice president of marketing. But, the
question that was being bounced around among whites in the wash-
rooms was whether this Black man would be accepted by the top-level
officials of the companies with which they were doing business. Gary
said:

There was a great deal of skepticism of whether or not I was the guy who actually had the authority of the company behind me. The implication was that I had the job but I didn't have the authority, which was obviously the furthest thing from the truth. The question that always hung in the air was, 'If I gave a price quote, would it stick?' I was tested many times in this regard. Questions were put to me and my answers were always challenged, but not directly. They would go behind my back and talk to my superiors, who would tell me what was being said. Every once in a while, the boss would actually call me into his office and put me through a step-by-step process to make sure the decisions that I had reached were not something I had pulled out of the air, but were based on sound business logic.

At this point in my career, I was as close to being indispensable as one could get but it never showed up in my pay raises. The last five pay increases I received were well below the compensation paid white executives performing at the same level. The fact that I was managing a $65 million annual budget and running close to 1,000 people made my job bigger than the jobs held by my peers in our industry nationwide. There is not a shadow of a doubt that I have been discriminated against.

If it were not for the racism against Blacks, I could have afforded to move to a smaller company and perhaps became the president and chief executive officer. A couple of whites working at a level below mine did leave and become heads of smaller companies.

The U.S. Army taught me what it meant to be Black, and I was never allowed to forget that lesson once I cast my net in the corporate sea.

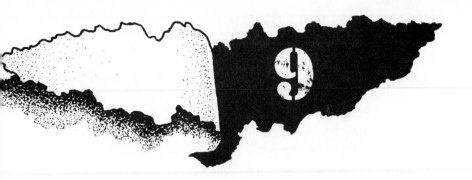

THE WHITE MEDIA IS NOT THE MESSAGE FOR BLACK AMERICANS

Benjamin Mumford was born July 10, 1944, on the military base at Fort Benning, Ga. His father had the rank of a full colonel in the U.S. Army, and he was frequently transferred from one Army installation to another. Ben lived in six states before he was 5 years old. The first housing that Ben can remember was integrated, the result of President Harry S. Truman's order to integrate the Army in 1949. Black and white officers lived in the same area but most Black enlisted men were still relegated to the ghetto sections of the Army bases until the mid-1950s.

Before young Ben reached school age, he had absorbed what most successful Blacks in corporate America must master to survive in today's market: the art of being bicultural. Young Mumford was as comfortable associating with his white playmates, who were the sons and daughters of Army officers, as he was when he went across the base to play with the kids of the Black enlisted men.

Benjamin attended a number of public schools while he was growing up. Some were populated by an all-white student body in his absence, and some of the other schools he attended were all Black. Sandwiched between the two extremes were a few integrated schools. The white students in non-integrated schools automatically assumed

Benjamin was a great athlete or an excellent dancer. Students in the Black schools made no assumptions, thus creating a nurturing and less-competitive climate for study. Ben's comfort level was at its highest when he was surrounded by Blacks, but he felt forced to be more competitive in the integrated schools. He knew that he was different, and that he was being watched. The integrated educational environment propelled him into becoming an overachiever. Benjamin made straight A's during his last two years in high school and graduated second in a class of 300 in a school that today would be described as a magnet school.

Ben Mumford arrived on the campus of Cornell University at Ithaca, N.Y., at just the right time politically. Between 1963 and 1967, Ben's extracurricular activities included getting arrested for participating in a demonstration for a Black studies program, participating in a free-speech movement sit-in and for leading protests against America's involvement in Vietnam. Benjamin graduated just two years before armed Black students in 1969 took over Cornell's Willard Straight Hall to protest the university's investment policy in South Africa.

On campus and in classrooms, Ben closely observed the white mentality. He found that white educators and administrators were essentially behind the front lines of corporate America. In the streets, he learned how the system really worked and what pressure and tactics to employ to change it.

Before Benjamin received a B.S. in political science, he had planned to attend Columbia University Law School in New York City. However, his experience in the politics of protest fostered an interest in journalism. Ben was appalled by the treatment the white media gave to Black news events. He wanted to start a long-overdue crusade to correct the wrongs the white media perpetuated. As an active Black student demonstrator, he chafed at the inaccurate coverage he received in the media. Ben felt that the demonstrations he had participated in were covered by white journalists who reported about another place and another time. Nothing has changed in 1990, and Ben still has his job cut out for him. Consider, for instance, the double-standard reporting that was done on the Howard Beach murder in New York City or the media circus that was created around Charles Stuart's grisly murder hoax in Boston, Mass.

Mumford's obsession with the power of the written word began with his immersion in John Steinbeck's "Grapes of Wrath," Richard

Wright's "Native Son," Ralph Ellison's "Invisible Man," Countee Cullen's "Copper Sun," and Walt Whitman's "Leaves of Grass." The propagandizing and distortion of the news by journalists of his day convinced Benjamin that he could use such language in action to tell his people what was really going on. The naive young man felt he was chosen to fill the big media void that existed in 1967, a void not filled to this day.

Mumford walked the streets of New York, Chicago and Boston for about nine months trying to hawk his talents to the barons of print journalism and television. Inevitably, he was told that without a journalism degree or any experience in the field, his chances of working in the media were nil. Finally tiring of hearing that he was not qualified, Benjamin enrolled as a communications major at Yale University, in New Haven, Conn. During the two years he spent learning the craft, he was never told about the dismal history of Black employment in the media nor advised that his chances of becoming a TV anchor person were slim to none.

Benjamin should have learned during his stay in the ivory tower that the Negro press was the only organ from 1865 through 1965 to advocate civil rights for Blacks. He should have learned that urban and rural newspapers, north and south, slanted their news to degrade Blacks—and that white composers wrote coon songs such as, "I Know Your Little Pickaninny Heart is White," to send a message to whites that Blacks are trivial, harmless and a hopeless lot. He also should have learned that metropolitan dailies did not begin to capitalize the word Negro until the late 1930s and early '40s and that "for colored only" ads for jobs and housing were commonplace through the 1950s.

Benjamin did observe that while the media may not have overtly promoted segregation, they covertly supported it by failing to object to the oppression of the Negro, hence bowing to the fear of losing white readership and advertisers. The Darkie Toothpaste ads promoted by Colgate-Pamolive Inc. in Asia for the past 60 years is a reprehensible example of how an American Fortune 500 company promoted the African-American image abroad. But Colgate does not stand alone: Lever Brothers Co. had its Golddust Twins cleanser, scouring and washing powder, and Quaker Oats used Aunt Jemima, a Black mammy caricature, to advertise its pancake product. The Aunt Jemima image has been updated over the past two decades to resemble a typical African-American housewife. "Little Black Sambo," first published in Great Britain in 1899, has been removed from many U.S. libraries, but is readily available in libraries and book stores in Japan; 20 editions of the story have been published in the past 35 years. Sanrio Company of Japan, which makes the offending "little Black Sambo" line of toys, and Sogo department stores, which display Black mannequins with enormous, grotesquely grinning mouths, question why Black Americans are offended by the stereotypes. And the beat goes on.

It was not until 1966, after years of litigation and organized protest by the NAACP and other civil rights groups, that the baboonery of Amos and Andy, Sapphire and Mama and other projections of Black life written, produced and directed by white men faded from the air waves and television screens. However, a 1990 screenplay has picked up the torch in the Academy award-winning Best Picture, "Driving Miss Daisy." Attorney Thomas N. Todd, the civil rights activist, eloquently observes:

> 'Driving Miss Daisy' is a subliminal message from white
> America indicating where they are most comfortable with
> Black people. They pine for this subjugated, quiet, non-
> confrontational, non-threatening, non-intimidating Black
> person. The demeanor of Morgan Freeman in his role as a
> chauffeur for Miss Daisy (played by the Academy award-
> winning Best Actress, Jessica Tandy) is how they really want
> to see and remember us. Whether we're working as
> executives in white corporate America, partners in a law
> office, doctors in hospitals or owning our own businesses,
> they want us driving Miss Daisy. The movie is a throwback
> to the 'good old times' when relationships between white
> people and Black people were clearly defined, with Blacks as
> subordinate and whites as superordinate. So Blacks approach
> the year 2000 where they began in 1900: driving Miss Daisy.

In contrast, Spike Lee's "Do The Right Thing" did not even get a whiff of an Oscar because it dealt with the racial realities of the 1990s, and was not softened by the emotional distance afforded by the yester-years. The 1990 Oscars mirror Hollywood's penchant to cast Blacks in the roles of standbys at their own funerals. Depicting the truth and dropping the stereotypes about Blacks would be a step forward in making America a living democracy.

The subordinate position of Blacks in America was not lifted by newspaper chains such as the one founded by William Randolph

Hearst and dailies like Col. Robert R. McCormick's *Chicago Tribune*, where patriotism and allegiance to the American flag were editorial priorities and where no attempts were made to persuade readers to adhere to the principles proclaimed by the 14th and 15th amendments of the American constitution. No white-owned metropolitan daily in the country, with the exception of the *Chicago Sun* when it was launched in 1941, made any noticeable effort to combat racial injustices and instill the right of racial equality. The general press ignored news of interest to Blacks until the events of Dr. Martin Luther King Jr.'s civil rights crusade and the charcoaling of American cities coalesced into a centerpiece of national attention.

The principal purpose of the print and the electronic media was to keep whites informed, and their broader coverage of the brutality of Sheriff Bull Conners, the Selma, Ala., boycott and the Birmingham, Ala., freedom riders proved to be an asset to the civil rights movement. Their reports acquainted many culturally isolated whites with the injustices being inflicted upon Black Americans whose ancestors had set foot on American soil before the arrival of the Mayflower.

Presidents John F. Kennedy and Lyndon Baines Johnson projected a spirit for racial fairness that caused television, radio and the print media to adopt a new attitude. The responsibility to offer fuller coverage caused the white press to begin to recognize the competence of Black newsmen as journalists and they began to raid Black newsrooms for their brightest and best writers. During the 1960s, Blacks were being shanghaied and placed by the media bosses into positions that generally were more visible than significant. The Federal Communications Commission began to enforce fair hiring policies. In 1965, Bill Matney and Mel Goode were selected as the first Blacks to be given national exposure as TV newsmen by the major networks.

Bill Matney, a fair-complexioned man, graduated from the University of Michigan in 1946. He had been a reporter and then managing editor with the *Michigan Chronicle*, in Detroit. He had been with the Chronicle 15 years before joining National Broadcast Communications (NBC), where he was assigned the White House beat.

Mel Goode, also a fair-skinned man, had a B.A. degree from the University of Pittsburgh. He had been a reporter for the *Pittsburgh Courier* for 14 years before going to work for American Broadcast Communications (ABC), where he was assigned to the United Nations.

Though it was suspected that Bill and Mel were intended as Black tokens—and they were—both were seasoned journalists whose credentials equaled or exceeded those of many of their white colleagues. Yet for all their qualifications and performance, they never advanced beyond their original assignments. Their appearance on television screens gradually diminished and, by 1972 had faded like water color paintings in the rain.

A hallmark in television arrived in 1978 when ABC named 39-year-old, tall, handsome, copper-colored Max Robinson, of Richmond, Va., its Chicago anchorman. Max added his booming baritone to the "World News Tonight" news team of Frank Reynolds in Washington and Peter Jennings in London. Never in the annals of television had a Black journalist been elevated to a permanent anchor spot in the highly competitive prime-time news period, a slot that generates the maximum amount of advertising dollars.

Frank Swertlow, television and radio critic for the *Chicago Sun-Times*, sought the reaction of television newsmen with whom Robinson would be competing locally. Some surprising responses surfaced: Bill Kurtis, top CBS Chicago anchorman, who had just negotiated a record $250,000 contract but hungered for the national exposure, opined that, "A Black anchorman standing in a wheat field in Kansas might not be able to relate to people in the Midwest. He's not gonna have any recognition in the Midwest. My God, I am stumped!"

"I am appalled at the idea that ABC is gonna send someone here to be a network anchorman. What expertise does he have?" asked Walter Jacobson, Kurtis' colleague at Chicago's CBS affiliate.

Advice for Robinson was forthcoming from Don Craig, a member of NBC's Chicago news team. He told the newcomer to, "Keep a low profile, be humble or Chicago will humiliate you." Don Craig did not know that it would be difficult to humiliate Max Robinson because, like Topsy, he entered television land through the back door.

Back in 1959, Max Robinson spotted a newspaper ad for a TV announcer in a Portsmouth, Va., newspaper. Those were the days of "help wanted" and "help wanted-C" ads with "C" meaning colored. Robinson answered even though it was not a "C" ad, and was hired to read the news behind a screen where he would be heard but not seen. One day he boldly told the crew to put him on camera. The flood of hostile phone calls resulted in his dismissal from the station. Thus was Max's television career launched in a place that, in his words, "wasn't ready for colored TV."

Television still wasn't ready by 1981, Mr. Robinson told an

audience at Smith College in North Hampton, Mass. On Sunday, February 8, Robinson compared the news media with "a crooked mirror" through which "white America views itself" and that "only by talking about racism or taking a professional risk will I take myself out of the mean, racist trap all Black Americans find themselves in."

A study released in 1989 by the Center for Media and Public Affairs revealed that there was still only one Black national network anchor, Carole Simpson, the weekend anchor for ABC. Ms. Simpson, a highly qualified journalist with more than 19 years of experience in television, holds a B.A. degree from the University of Michigan and a master's of journalism from the University of Iowa. Even today, despite the abundance of talented Blacks on local television stations throughout the country, they have had few opportunities to make an impact behind the screens where corporate decisions dictate program directions.

The print media selected not to publicize the addition of Blacks to their editorial staffs. Unlike Black television personalities, Black journalists remain as hidden as most Black radio personalities.

A Black reporter working for a white Chicago daily in the 1950s was one of the best-kept secrets in town. The late Enoc Waters, former executive editor of the *Chicago Defender*, recalled in *American Diary*, a personal history of the Black press:

A Black reporter was dispatched to a news conference at the Sherman Hotel (which was located on the present site of the State of Illinois Building.) As he was about to enter the conference room, the newsman was challenged by a white public relations official standing at the door passing out press kits and greeting the media folk as they arrived.

'What do you want?' the official asked abruptly.

'I am a reporter,' responded the Black man, a little startled by the unfriendly reception. The public relations official's racist mindset had caused him to misunderstand the reporter and he exclaimed loudly, 'Porter? We didn't call for a porter.'

Although upset by the hostile attitude, the reporter tried to clarify his status. 'I didn't say I am a porter . . .,' he began, but he was interrupted in mid-sentence by another question.

'Then what are you doing here?'

The Black man bellowed, 'I am a reporter, a newsman, a journalist. Do you understand?'

Surprised by the Black man's anger, and his loud response, the white PR man nudged the Black man into the hall and asked apologetically, 'Whom do you represent?'

When the reporter informed him that he represented the largest paper in Chicago, the PR man responded, 'I didn't know they had any colored reporters. I'm awfully sorry. Why didn't somebody tell me?'

The silent conspiracy that accompanied the employment of Blacks by the white press aroused the curiosity of the Black newspaper owners from whom the reporters had been hired. Did the white editors fear the reaction of white readers? Would making such an announcement indicate a change in the employment policy and be an admission that merit rather than color was a factor for hiring Black reporters? Would white reporters feel slighted by such announcements, which had not been routine when they had been hired? Had opening the doors of the fourth estate proven to be the millennium for Black reporters?

Were Blacks fulfilled by the opportunities to work for the metropolitan press, opportunities in the form of better working conditions, increased salaries and an expanded forum? The answer was yes, yes, yes! Thus, many observers were surprised when several excellent Black writers like Wallace Terry at *Time*, Sam Yette at *Newsweek* and Lu Palmer at the *Chicago Daily News*, deserted their desks in the white media heaven.

The reality of working for the white press had fallen short of their expectations. Their disillusionment did not rise from dissatisfaction with working conditions or salaries but with the oppression of the white editors who continued to rewrite the truth out of their stories as they saw it.

Most Blacks find it almost impossible to separate their Black experience from their jobs. Writers are more sensitive than many people, and Black writers are super sensitive as a result of their track record in the United States. Some Blacks find it impossible to function as an unemotional technician without reacting as Blacks to the events that they report.

There was a definite conflict between how some Blacks wanted to use the media that issued their paychecks and how they were required to use it by their white editors. Some journalists eased their discomfort by writing anonymously for Black newspapers or liberal community publications. Sam Yette lowered his blood pressure by authoring a revolutionary book entitled, *The Choice* when he worked for *News-week*. The search for fairness and the spirit to crusade for Black causes did not die in the hearts and minds of some Black writers simply because they changed jobs.

Civil rights activist Lu Palmer changed jobs and continued his commitment to Black empowerment. Palmer, an excellent writer with a B.A. degree from Virginia Union, Richmond, Vir., and a M.A. from Syracuse University, Syracuse, N.Y., left the *Chicago Daily Defender* in 1966 for the *Daily News*, where he remained from 1966 to 1972. Lu's expectations of a big pay raise, greater exposure and prestige were realized. But he discovered that the freedom of expression for a Black columnist was restricted by racism. The dedication to justice and equality that permeated the *Chicago Daily Defender*'s newsroom were reflected in the *Daily News* editorials only when whites felt their rights had been violated.

Palmer had many disagreements with his bosses over editorial judgements. Some were vocalized, but most were internalized. The climax came in 1972 after Palmer wrote a column condemning the police brutality against Blacks. The Chicago police on December 4, 1969, had raided an apartment at 2337 W. Monroe St., and shot to death Fred Hampton and Mark Clark, two members of the Black Panther Party. The young men were unarmed and asleep in their beds. Palmer was aroused by the refusal of local officials to respond to Black demands for an explanation of police conduct. Palmer's column ignited the fireworks that had threatened to explode the comfortable editorial policy at the *Daily News*.

The column was rejected by his editor on the grounds that it might not be understood by the white readers who constituted 80 percent of the paper's circulation. Palmer resigned and formed his own news-paper, the *Black X Express*. Palmer's paper failed, as did the *Daily News* several years later because of decreasing circulation. "I was foolish to think that the *Daily News* or any other white-controlled publication would allow me to use their facility to fight the racism that undergirds the structure of their support," Palmer said later.

Vernon Jarrett, a member of the *Chicago Sun-Times* editorial board, newspaper columnist and TV host, raised the question, "How Black should a Black journalist be?" and argued:

Communicators can lose all consideration of integrity, not to mention craftsmanship and trip over themselves by trying

to march to someone else's drummer. The best approach for
any newsman—regardless of race—is to report and
interpret the world with a sensitivity based upon one's own
history, learning and perspective. There is nothing wrong
with trying to put one's self in another's shoes. Empathy is
a core ingredient of civilized conduct.

Robert Maynard, a former *Washington Post* reporter became the
first Black owner of a major metropolitan newspaper, when he bought
the *Oakland Tribune*. He explains the ambivalence of a Black newsman in a white newsroom this way, "You start off with a regard for
your culture and your community and you bring this along to work. The
problem is that many white editors say, 'Okay, you start over there with
a view of yourself. I start over here with a view that is very different. If
you want to work here, *you* got to cross the bridge.'"

Wallace Terry, Sam Yette and Lu Palmer attempted to walk across
the white man's bridge only to discover at midpoint that they had to
turn back. The toll that "the man" asked them to pay in Black pride and
Black self-determination was more than they were willing to sur-
render.

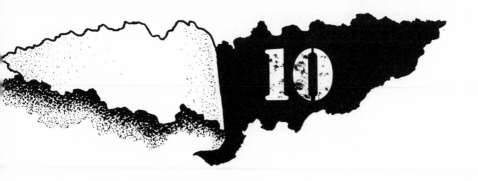

AMERICA'S UNEMPLOYABLES: YOUNG, BLACK AND HIGHLY EDUCATED

Willard Mays was born May 25, 1955, on a reservation located at 4428 S. Calumet Ave., on the South Side of Chicago. Willard was the eldest of two children raised in the core section of the ghetto and in the midst of shelters for the underclass. Their parents Mary Belle and Joshua, were migrant sharecroppers from Mississippi. The Mays were not formally educated, but they were very nurturing and supportive, continually communicating ideas of hope and grandness to Willard and his sister.

Willard's earliest remembrance was the roar of the El trains, which sounded as though they passed through his bedroom around the clock, though the El tracks were approximately 150 feet from his bedroom window. The thundering of the Jackson Park Express and the Englewood El rocked Willard to sleep like a lullaby, and the little boy grew up fascinated by the magic of elevator tracks that supported the trains and permitted them to rattle, rock and roll without falling. Willard tried to duplicate the elevated tracks with matches, match boxes, hair pins, rocks or whatever he could find that would make his imaginary El tracks stand erect.

The lad carried his daydream of building an El train and tracks right into kindergarten at the Forrestville Elementary School, where he experimented with building elevated railroad tracks using Tinkertoys.

Willard was so bored in Chicago's public elementary schools that he became a problem for his teachers. Several weeks before he graduated from grammar school, he decided that he wanted to attend the prestigious St. Ignatius High School on West Roosevelt Road in Chicago, but he was discouraged by his teachers because of his behavioral problems. The teachers told Willard that he would have difficulty getting into the school because of his poor economic background and because he was not Catholic. The boy ignored the advice of the naysayers and, to their surprise, passed the entrance exam at St. Ignatius with a score that placed him near the top of the freshman class. His success caused young Willard to question the judgment of the teachers who had downplayed his ability and intensified his appreciation for the encouragement provided by his mother and father, who never stopped telling him that he was a world-class achiever.

Willard was astonished and overjoyed to discover that the Catholic school allowed him to own his textbooks. In the Chicago public schools, teachers distributed textbooks at the beginning of the class and collected them at the end of the period, denying students the privilege of further study at home. Willard was unable to take even one book home during the eight years he spent in public schools. At St. Ignatius, he was allowed to take his books home, even write in their margins, and for the first time develop good study habits. The catalysts who gored him into more intensive study were not the priests or nuns but two students who always got better grades than his, even though Willard felt they were not as bright as he. To outdo those two students, Willard checked out and devoured books recommended in the textbooks, and blossomed into a "straight A" student in physics, chemistry and mathematics. By the end of his junior year, Willard dared to dream of going to college on a scholarship or with the assistance of a loan.

Young Mays, emboldened by his 3.9 grade point average, applied to the Massachusetts Institute of Technology (MIT), Cambridge, Mass. The alumnus who interviewed Willard Mays as part of the MIT screening process worked in an office at 69 W. Washington, Chicago. Willard vividly remembers their meeting:

> The palms of my hands and my armpits became sweaty the
> moment I stepped on the elevator in the Brunswick
> Building and pushed the button that would permit me to
> exit on the sixth floor. I had not gotten comfortably seated
> in the MIT alum's office when he walked in and pulled

down a shade. On the inside of the shade was a complete periodic table blown up. The table was all abbreviations and numbers. After asking me some preliminary questions, he said, 'Why don't you go down this periodic table and recite every element on the table that you recognize?' Fortunately, I was familiar with every element on the table. When I finished, he smiled and said, 'It seems to me as though you understand this table quite well.' He continued the interview for maybe an hour and a half, although it seemed like forever. Toward the end, he queried: 'Do you have a lab in your basement? Did you play with chemistry sets when you were in grammar school?'

I told him we didn't have a basement in the 75-year-old kitchenette apartment building owned by a white landlord who lived in a luxury condominium on North Lake Shore Drive. There was no place for me to experiment with chemicals except the kitchen sink, and my mother would not have tolerated that.

At the conclusion of the interview, he told me I was a very bright boy and that I should do well in life. However, he said, he could not recommend me to MIT because he felt that I did not have a strong enough science background.

Upon hearing that, my feathers fell but I maintained a stoic posture. Our parents had taught my sister and me a lot of self restraint. I had sat through that interview docile and respectful, and had said nothing that could have been interpreted as offensive. However, after I left his office enroute home, the further I got away from him, the angrier I became. By the time I reached the Wabash Avenue El platform, I was fuming. And when I finally reached my third-floor apartment on the reservation, I was angry enough to eat a cockroach.

In spite of that negative experience, I wasn't disheartened. I said to myself, if that alumnus was the kind of person they choose to represent MIT, I'd better look around for a university that will recognize my potential. My other choices for engineering schools were the Illinois Institute of Technology, Chicago, and the University of Illinois at Urbana.

I made the decision to go to Urbana because they offered

me an academic scholarship. I joined the track team one year but had to give it up. It was just too much work running 10 months a year and trying to make good grades. Chemical engineering turned out to be a bit harder to digest than I had expected. I had thought I was pretty bright because I usually could take information home, work on it, stay up all night and get the right answers.

In the Chemical Engineering 100 class, they gave assignments that were so difficult that I would stare at the problems all night long and still not come up with a solution. I couldn't figure out heads or tails of the material, yet, the next day, I'd walk into the classroom and find everybody was turning in their homework assignments except me.

I found out that many of my white classmates depended on their fraternity brothers to supply fact sheets and old tests going back to Columbus. The information that the brothers furnished was just what a young, struggling student needed to lighten the load. The white boys didn't share any information with me. After all, I didn't belong to any of their fraternities and I was the only Black in the class.

Before too many days passed, I discovered there were other groups holding study sessions. Until then, I thought I was the only chemical engineering major on campus trying to go it alone. To survive in the program, I tried hanging with the independent study groups, but they wouldn't tolerate me for very long. When I began to get signals that I had worn out my welcome, I just moved on to another study group and I was able to at least get my assignments done on time.

Crashing the various study groups was my first lesson in melting, that is edging myself into situations where I wasn't necessarily welcome. My persistence paid off and I graduated with a B average and a bachelor's degree in chemical engineering.

My first job after finishing college was with the UAWM Corporation selling chemicals. I found working in sales interesting because when you were out in the field, that's where you really tended to show your worth as an individual. If you're a good salesman, your superiors are not gonna bother you much. You're pretty much your own boss as long as you're meeting the quotas. All my clients were white but they didn't give me any problems because they needed our products. They were always happy to see me coming as long as I didn't cause them to lose any money, and I didn't.

After five years at UAWM, I knew I didn't want to sell chemicals the rest of my life and I decided to seek a master's degree in business administration. My bosses disagreed with me and basically said that I didn't need an MBA at that particular point in my career. When I told them I was applying to the Kellogg School of Business at Northwestern University, Chicago, and would be taking advantage of the tuition reimbursement program, they transferred me to the headquarters office in the east with the promise of a promotion. The "promotion" turned out to be a position as recruiter for college graduates for the different divisions of the company. The extensive traveling involved in recruiting made the job very interesting for a while, but after two years, problems began. All of a sudden it was clear that the promotion that I had been promised was not going to come about. I had expected to be appointed to a slot as a business analyst, which would enable me to be directly involved in accounting. For reasons that I can't put my finger on, I was discouraged from seeking this type of assignment. I was delighted when I learned that I had been accepted at the Kellogg School of Business and arranged to get reassigned to Chicago. For about three years, I basically traveled three days a week on the job and took two night classes. UAWM management weren't as supportive of my aggressive schedule as I would have liked for them to be. Their general conception was that because I was Black, single, in sales and going to school at night, I couldn't possibly be able to balance everything at once. They also assumed that I was chasing every skirt in sight, which was the furthest thing from the truth. They figured something had to suffer and it wasn't skirt chasing, it must have been the job. No matter how good my professional performance, they wanted more. They put all of my activities under intense scrutiny.

The chemical industry went into a down turn in 1983.

The big bosses then decided to structure me out and bring in
a young white boy as sales manager, a position that I
rightfully merited on education, experience and
performance. The fellow they promoted did not have a
chemical engineering degree and was not enrolled in any
graduate program. He had no knowledge of the company
and I did. Moreover, I had to train him. His loaded gun was
being white and having a friend in the hierarchy.

  After I was passed over for the management position, I
opted out of the company under what they call a surplus
program, where they surplus my job and thereby enable me
to leave the company whole. They also agreed to bridge my
pension so I could receive immediately the full benefits that
were due me at the end of the year. I gave the company an
"A" for its separation bonus.

Willard Mays would have never separated from his job if he had
known what it was like out in the streets. He had been fortunate
enough to graduate from the University of Illinois in the early 1970s
when Black was still beautiful, and white firms were recruiting qualified Blacks because they were in style. In 1980, when Ronald Reagan
was elected president of the United States, the job scene began to
change dramatically. Conservatives on the Supreme Court worked
with all deliberate speed to turn the civil rights clock back to syn-
chronize with the dismal pre-1960 times.

  After more than a year of looking for employment, Willard was
sick of hearing that he was overqualified for every job he sought.
Potential employers discouraged him: "You don't want this job. This
job is beneath you. You wouldn't be satisfied with this job. I'm sure you
wouldn't be interested." Willard tried to impress upon them that he
was willing to take on lesser jobs. He had a family to feed and a house
note to pay, but his pleas fell on deaf ears. Willard believes that the
current hue and cry about the work force 2000 is nothing but propaganda pumped out by the same corporations that are turning qualified
Blacks down for jobs in work force 1990.

  A vice president of a Fortune 500 corporation seemed prepared to
offer Willard a job at a starting salary of $45,000 a year, plus a car.
However, after reviewing Mays' resume a second time, the vp had
second thoughts. "You are worth more than $45,000 based on what I
see here. You are overqualified for the position I had in mind," he told

Willard. While the man explained that he didn't think that the job would be challenging enough for Mays, Willard was bellowing, "Give me a break." Today, after 18 months of job hunting, Willard has not had a single bona fide job offer.

Letters A through I are samples of the 62 rejections Willard has received from major corporations in the past 12 months. Willard, who does not drink, smoke or use hard drugs, who played the corporate game by company rules, was thrown into the scrap heap of the unemployables before he reached his 35th birthday.

The following letters have not been paraphrased. They are accurate to the period. All are from Fortune 500 companies. We have omitted the names of the corporations and the writers' signatures in the hope that there may be a change of policy that would enable the corporate fathers to find some "right fits" between their needs and Willard's qualifications.

LETTER A

Corporation ZY

July 13, 1989

Mr. Willard Mays
5300 S. St. Lawrence
Chicago, IL 60600

Dear Mr. Mays:

We certainly enjoyed your visit and I feel that you have much to offer a company such as (the company).

At this time, there is no readily apparent fit between our current openings and your interests and background. We are, however, circulating your resume among managers who may have openings in the near term. Should an appropriate opportunity occur, we will contact you promptly.

Willard, we appreciate your interest in (the company) and wish you the best in your career search.

Sincerely,

Manager, Corporate Placement

P.S. Willard, I'd like to make something happen, but at this time there's just not the right fit.

LETTER B

Corporation AD

December 13, 1989

Mr. Willard Mays
5300 S. St. Lawrence
Chicago, IL 60600

Dear Mr. Mays:

My survey of employment opportunities for you is now complete and, with regret, I must inform you that we are unable to develop a suitable position.

The primary consideration in the hiring of new employees is to place them in a challenging position that offers growth potential within our company. Your background, qualifications and work interest were carefully reviewed against our immediate employment needs and, unfortunately, we were unable to find an appropriate match at this time.

Naturally, I am very sorry that we cannot be more encouraging, and I extend my best wishes for success in your professional pursuits.

We appreciate your interest in (the company).

Sincerely,

PROFESSIONAL STAFFING
SECTION

College Relations Supervisor

LETTER C

Corporation PX

September 22, 1989

Mr. Willard Mays
5300 S. St. Lawrence
Chicago, IL 60600

Dear Mr. Mays:

Thank you for your interest in employment opportunities with (the company).

Your resume is being made available to a professional employment network so that it can be reviewed against current job openings nationwide. This will ensure you the broadest possible consideration within (the company).

Due to our diverse business needs, we do not use a centralized approach to employment. You would hear directly from the organization with the opportunity, should your background and qualifications so suggest. Your resume will remain actively available to our employment network for 90 days.

On behalf of (the company) I would like to express our appreciation that you included us in your job search. We wish you well in your career pursuits.

Sincerely,

University Relations Director

LETTER D

Corporation CS

October 2, 1989

Mr. Willard Mays
5300 S. St. Lawrence
Chicago, IL 60600

Dear Mr. Mays:

I have received your resume and have reviewed it in light of our current openings.

Based on this review, I am unable to discuss a position with you which would be appropriate for someone with your background. If a position would become available within the near future, someone from my office will contact you.

Thank you for your interest in (the company), and good luck in your job search.

Sincerely,

Vice President
Director of Human Resources

LETTER E

Corporation QA

September 15, 1989

Willard Mays
5300 S. St. Lawrence
Chicago, IL 60600

Dear Mr. Mays:

Thank you for your interest in (the company).

Your resume shows many fine qualities, unfortunately we are looking for someone with a slightly different background.

We wish you the best of luck in finding a new position.

Sincerely,

Manager-Regional Data Center

LETTER F

Corporation BN

July 14, 1989

Willard Mays
5300 S. St. Lawrence
Chicago, IL 60600

Dear Mr. Mays:

Thank you for your recent visit to the offices of (the corporation) to discuss career opportunities with (the corporation). We appreciate your taking the time to consider employment opportunities with our company.

At (the company) we place great emphasis on matching an applicant's background with the requirements of our current job openings. After reviewing our present hiring needs and your qualifications, we find we are unable to further pursue the employment you are seeking.

We appreciate your thinking of our company and wish you success in finding a rewarding position.

Sincerely

Human Resources
General Office

LETTER G

Corporation DW

July 3, 1989

Mr. Willard Mays
5300 S. St. Lawrence
Chicago, IL 60600

Dear Mr. Mays:

Thank you for your expression of interest in employment with (the company).

We have given careful consideration to your inquiry and reviewed your stated qualifications against our current employment needs. Despite all you might have to offer, we simply do not, at this time, have a position which we feel is appropriate.

Again, your interest in (the company) is appreciated.

Sincerely,

Vice President
Human Resources

LETTER H

Corporation RG

November 22, 1989

Mr. Willard Mays
5300 S. St. Lawrence
Chicago, IL 60600

Dear Mr. Mays:

Thank you for your interest in (the corporation). I enjoyed meeting you at the Black MBA Convention in Chicago. I am glad that we had the opportunity to discuss possible employment with our organization.

We are in the process of reviewing your background and experience against our current and projected needs. This process takes time, so do not interpret the lack of immediate response as a rejection. If we do not have an immediate position available that is commensurate with your interests, we would like to retain your resume in our active files as we are expanding and undertaking new markets. Should an appropriate position become available, we hope you will still be interested in discussing employment possibilities with our company.

Again, your interest in employment opportunities with (the corporation) is appreciated.

Sincerely yours,

Director, Human Resources

LETTER I

Corporation EA

October 24, 1989

Willard Mays
5300 S. St. Lawrence
Chicago, IL 60600

Dear Mr. Mays:

Thank you for your interest in a position with (the company).

We have thoroughly reviewed your credentials and though they are most impressive, regret to inform you we cannot offer further encouragement at this time.

We appreciate your interest and offer best wishes in your search for suitable employment.

Sincerely,

Employment Manager

The letters of rejection received by Willard Mays are so similar in tone and content that they raise the spectre of corporate officers from across the country gathered in back rooms deciding on a common kinder and gentler language for rejecting qualified Black applicants. Such gatherings could be called a conspiracy and it is undeniable that such schemes are in place.

Major corporations are hiring employment agencies to do the dirty work for them, dirty work concealed in elaborate code. Robert Abrams, attorney general of New York state, leads an ongoing investigation of a number of employment agencies of that type. He says that the message conveyed to prospects by the agencies imply, "If you want to do well here, you want to earn some money, don't send minorities for the good, top jobs. Don't send Black people who are going to be visible out front as receptionists, or to be the executive secretary to the president of a major company or corporation." Agencies couch that message in a language all their own, Mr. Abrams found.

Attorney General Abrams states, "It's a pretty deep entrenched system where people know what the rules of the game are and they actually have a code to implement those rules." Some internal application cards are marked with codes like "FOA," which means a white person with a front office appearance. A corporation tells an employment agency that it is looking for an All-American. That means that they want a white, preferably blonde with blue eyes, but most definitely white. The request for a "corporate" in the employment agency code means the applicant must have skin color that will fit into a predominantly white corporate environment. The codes disguise illegal discrimination and ensure that no minorities, no matter how qualified, would be recommended for jobs reserved for whites.

CBS sent out two employees, one Black and one white, to do job testing at Cosmopolitan Personnel Systems, New York. The Black woman was called Miriam Marx, and the white woman assumed the name of Lorraine Davis. "Miriam" received no recommendations, although she can type 72 words per minute with three errors. "Lorraine," who could type only 62 words a minute with 15 mistakes, was offered several jobs. Interviewers told the white woman that she was the "corporate type" and scheduled interviews for her at three prestigious firms.

Shortly after CBS' "60 Minutes" finished filming this story, which was televised Feb. 11, 1990, Attorney General Abrams issued subpoenas for all personnel records at Cosmopolitan's Manhattan office.

RICHARD LINYARD: THE MAN WHO LIFTED HIMSELF FROM PORTER TO PRESIDENT

Richard Linyard was born in Maywood, Ill., October 24, 1930, exactly one year after the great stock market crash of 1929. The country was descending into a deep and prolonged economic depression. President Herbert C. Hoover, in a fevered attempt to keep the faith with those who had become accustomed to eating high off of the hog of the roaring '20s, was promising every American of voting age two chickens in every pot and one car in every garage. Three popular tunes that captured the somber mood of that year were, "On the Sunny Side of the Street," by Dorothy Fields and Jimmy McHugh, "Love for Sale," by Cole Porter and "Get Happy," by Ted Koehler and Harold Arlen.

The Linyards were a lucky, happy family. Charles, Richard's father, chauffeured for a wealthy white family who lived in Oak Park, Ill. Although Charles' salary was meager, his wife Nonela managed it well. Richard, the youngest of the Linyard's 10 children, received a lot of advice from his siblings along with their hand-me-down clothes. He did not own a new suit until he was 17 years old. He purchased that suit for his high school graduation with money he had earned as a *Chicago Tribune* paper boy.

After Richard graduated from Proviso High in Maywood, Ill., in 1947, he got a job working as a porter at the Bond Clothing Store in

Oak Park. Among his duties was washing the store's outside showcase windows several times a week. He usually performed this chore shortly after daybreak, before the street traffic got heavy. Richard recalls some astonishing developments:

> A white gentleman, enroute to work across the street at the Oak Park Trust and Savings Bank, would often stop and chat with me for a few minutes as I washed the windows. Ernest Wagner, the vice president of the bank, frequently signed my $2 money order checks when I went to the bank on Fridays. One day while he was signing my money order, Mr. Wagner told me, 'We've got a very fine colored janitorial force working here. How would you like to work for us when we get an opening?'
>
> I said, 'Fine,' because I felt that I would make more money at the bank than I was making at the clothing store. After about six months had passed, Mr. Wagner called me and said, 'You remember we spoke about a job over here.'
>
> I said, 'Yes.'
>
> He said, 'I want you to stop by and talk to me about it. I know that you only make $98 a month over there, and we pay $198 a month here. Would you be interested?'
>
> I said, 'My goodness, yes I would be.'
>
> I started working at the bank a week after I was offered the job. My janitorial duties included operating the passenger elevator 2½ hours every evening. I saw that portion of my job as an opportunity to observe the bank customers and employees at a close range. I used to see the directors of the bank come in and out of the building. I got to know them by name and they knew me as the man with a pleasant smile. One day, after a bank board meeting and just before it was time to close the elevators down, Ellis Denny, the president of the bank, entered the elevator. 'I'd like to talk to you,' he said, and sat on the little chair at the rear of the elevator. He rode up and down with me as we talked for better than 15 minutes. I mentioned during the course of the conversation that a lot of the white kids I went to school with at Proviso High School were working in the bank. And since I had the same training and academic background, I would like to do something other than janitorial work. In

fact, I told him I would like a white-collar job in the bank.'

'Let me give that some thought,' Mr. Denny replied.

A month later, they fired the regular elevator operator and offered the job to me. They wanted to know if I'd take it. I said of course. They said, 'We like the way you handle the customers that come in and out of our building. You are cordial and friendly. We appreciate that. Consider your new position as a fulltime elevator operator as your first promotion.'

I did not learn until later that the president had put me on the center elevator so he could watch me. My elevator stopped directly in front of his office on the second floor. About two months after I became a fulltime elevator operator, the president said, 'There's a school that we send our people to and I think it would be nice for you to go.'

I said, 'I would be grateful for the opportunity.'

When the American Institute of Banking sent me their registration card, they had no idea I was Negro. The first night I showed up for class and they saw that I was Black, there were looks of both surprise and shock on everybody's face. The administrator of the school called the president of the bank the first thing the next morning and yelled, 'We have never had a Negro here.' Remember, this is 1955. 'Well, you have one now,' the bank president rejoined and slammed down the telephone.

The most embarrassing thing in my life happened to me the second night of class. I said if I ever taught school, I would never let what happened to me happen to anybody else.

At the beginning of class, the teacher asked everyone to stand and give their name, where they worked and what they did. The students rose one by one, gave their names, the institutions that they worked for and the departments they worked in such as trust, credit department, bookkeeping, etc. When it came my turn, I said my name is Richard Linyard and I am an elevator operator at the Oak Park Trust and Savings Bank. Everybody looked at me with big grins on their faces and started to laugh. They laughed and they laughed. It seemed to me like they must have laughed for hours. I was so humiliated that I could have jumped into a six-foot grave and buried myself without any assistance. However, I got the last laugh because I received the second highest grade in that class at the end of the term.

I was so elated about my good grade that I could hardly wait until I got to the bank. As I piloted the elevator, I showed my report card to everyone I thought might be interested in my progress. I thought everybody else would be as elated as I was. I was dead wrong.

A trust officer by the name of Elliott rained on my parade. He looked at my report card and said, 'Richard, that's great. But a lot of good it's going to do you here.' Then he threw the report card on the elevator floor, and stepped on it when he got off.

Elliott was a cold and crude man, but he was right based on the history of the bank. However, he had no idea that the president of the bank perceived me as someone with the aspiration to be something other than an elevator operator.

President Denny wanted me to be exposed to the right people and made sure that I was the only operator who worked late on the nights the board of directors met. He also saw to it that I was scheduled to work extra hours whenever they had stockholder's meetings. When we held open house in our new building, he asked me to be one of the guides. He was showcasing me without making a verbal declaration.

Finally, one day he said, 'We got another opening at the bank and we'd like to have you try out for the job.' So, I got my first white-collar job in 1956, when I was promoted to a bookkeeper. On my first day in the bookkeeping department, I heard one of the white bank officers tell the lady who was training me to give me a hard time. He had no idea that I overheard him. However, the woman saw me over his shoulders, and later that day told me she was not gonna be a part the conspiracy to keep me from learning the job.

One day after I had been in bookkeeping for a couple of months, I stopped by President Denny's office to thank him for the job.

'I know I'm limited here, but I think . . .,' I began but before I could finish the sentence, he interrupted me:

'You're only limited by your own ability. That's all there is to that.'

He kept his word. The next thing I knew, I was promoted to the position of teller. The seven tellers were white women, some attractive, some not. The older ones would not do anything to help me. I struggled for several weeks trying to learn that job and praying that I would not make too many mistakes. Finally, a young teller from Birmingham, Ala., came over to my station and said, 'Richard, I'm not supposed to do this but I'm gonna help you. I don't care what they think.'

She was an excellent teller and teacher. Her assistance was paramount in helping me increase my competence and confidence on the job in a relatively short period of time.

The teller duties ceased to be a challenge to Richard once he was properly introduced to the mechanics of the job. President Denny recognized this and within seven months promoted the young man to a position where his responsibilities included consolidating the bank's accounts and compiling its daily financial report.

Richard Linyard's career path is significant when you consider that he had not set foot inside of a college or university. He found a mentor in Ellis Denny, a man who was an equal opportunity trailblazer. At that time, the only other Blacks in metropolitan Chicago with similar job exposure were Norman Simon at the Exchange National Bank and Walter Brewster at Main Bank. Both were college graduates.

President Denny wouldn't let any grass grow under Richard's feet. Richard remembers:

Back in those days, the board of directors met and elected new officers after the annual stockholders' meeting. There was a tradition at the bank that those aspiring to be officers would stay close to the phone until 10 or 11:00 p.m., hoping to get a call. Lucky for me I got a call from President Denny, who said, 'Congratulations, you have just become an officer at Oak Park Trust. You will be assistant manager in our savings department.'

I was enraptured and my family shared my joy. I had been appointed a bank officer at age 30. I know plenty of people who have worked for 25 years in banks and never made officer. With my new title came the authority to sign checks and other documents. It really was a great opportunity for me. In my case, receiving advice and encouragement from Mr. Denny, in addition to working hard, bore fruit.

Richard was more than pleased with his progress during his 14 years with Oak Park Trust. He planned to stay with the bank 11 more years and become eligible for a pension at age 45. Since he considered 45 years of age too young to retire, he targeted the post office as his next career move. He planned to be there for 20 years and draw two pensions when he retired at age 65.

By his own admission, Richard's vision was limited until a group of investors, headed by the late Ernest Collins, confided to him that they were organizing to open a Black-owned bank on the South Side of Chicago. Richard was excited by the possibilities because he had more bank experience than any other Black at the time, except Norman Simon at Exchange National, Walter Brewster at Main Bank, and Corky Lott at the South Side Bank and Trust Company. On the other hand, several blacks had had extensive experience in the savings and loan industry. Louise Quarles had a high profile at Illinois Federal Savings & Loan Association, where she later became president. Henry P. Hervey at the Service Federal Savings and Loan Association became president of the newly-organized Independence Bank of Chicago.

There had been no black bank presidents in Chicago since the 1930s when Jesse Binga was the chief executive officer at the Binga State Bank and attorney Richard Hill served in the same capacity at the Douglas National Bank. Although Linyard was not offered the top post at the new bank, he believed there was a real possibility he could eventually become president of the new institution.

Richard reluctantly left the Oak Park Trust and Savings Bank to join the Seaway National Bank of Chicago as cashier in 1964. His progress at Seaway was steady: he was promoted to vice president of cashiers, then to executive vice president and was subsequently appointed president in 1973.

Richard Linyard had implicit confidence in Ellis Denny, his mentor at Oak Park Bank, but he knew in his heart and head that there was not even a remote possibility of becoming the president of that institution or any other white-owned bank. There were too many white boys in the line ahead of him.

SOME EXPERIENCES IN THE LIFE OF DANIEL BOWMAN AS HE ASCENDS TO THE PRESIDENCY OF A WHITE ASSOCIATION

Daniel Bowman was born into a middle-class family in Atlanta, Ga., January 10, 1931, the only child of parents who were teachers in the city's public school system. His father Edmond was a graduate of Morehouse College in Atlanta, and his mother Lucinda received her undergraduate degree in elementary education from Spelman College on the same campus. Young Bowman received a bachelor's degree from his dad's alma mater, a master's from Columbia University, New York, and a doctorate from Harvard University, Cambridge, Mass.

Daniel can best be described as bright but not arrogant, reserved but not docile or timid. He is a large man who moves with the pace and grace of a ballet dancer. Most white folks would consider him a non-threatening Negro, and there were no objections when he joined a practically all-white professional association early in his career. Bowman remembers some of the meetings during his first year:

> I didn't know anybody in my subchapter. They always met at
> the Mayflower Hotel. I always had a feeling of discomfort
> when I walked into that lobby because I knew that Negroes
> had not historically been welcome as guests. The
> management probably made an exception in my case

because of the prestige of the association and must have
been forewarned that the group was expecting one colored
fellow. I always approached the table where I was going to
sit with great trepidation because I was afraid no one would
talk to me. Frequently that was the case. I would just sit
there like Humpty Dumpty, feeling worse than he did when
he fell off of the wall. Occasionally, someone would be
decent enough to speak to me. As time passed, I was
intermittently invited to participate in the table
conversations. Some of the people were just plain cruel;
they would shift conversations to topics they assumed I
could not comment on. I interpreted their behavior as a
deliberate effort to isolate me and let me know that I didn't
belong, but I was determined to stick it out. After about a
year, more and more of the guys sought my friendship and
seemed to respect some of my views. Other Blacks who
were members of the association did not attend the
meetings at the Mayflower. They just didn't want to go
through that crap. I endured the silence and humiliation
knowing that it was a fiery furnace to test my faith.

Daniel Bowman's stoic behavior built a responsible image that
eased his rise to the presidency of the organization. He had no adver-
sarial relationship with anyone in the group. There was no organized
opposition to his movement through the various elective offices.
Although the positions were not handed to him on a silver platter, he
never endured the animosity that thwarts quasi-militant Blacks who
aspire to become heads of white-controlled professional organizations.
Bowman was the right man at the right time.

Bowman decided to become a candidate for president of his association almost 20 years before he reached the first rung on the officer's
ladder. He began his move toward the top by taking on thankless tasks
that no one else wanted. Many of these administrative "housekeeping"
chores were at the lowest levels, levels that no one could possibly envy.
Though he tackled each assignment with the vigor of a star quarter-
back, he never gave out any threatening signals. Daniel willingly
labored in the vineyards and never stood around waiting for applause.

Rewards for Bowman's hard-working, no-nonsense approach
were a long time coming. He was elected sergeant at arms, which was
one step above mascot, shortly after his 19th anniversary with the

organization. Moving up the organizational ladder was relatively easy once he got his foot on the bottom rung. From that point, it was almost automatic—almost because in previous years two Blacks had been toppled off the ladder on the second and third rungs. Daniel was patient and climbed rung by rung, mending fences when necessary, before finally reaching the presidency.

Bowman almost jumped off the association ladder when he moved up to treasurer. When he learned that as treasurer he would have to write checks to a lobbyist who was an avowed racist, his first reaction was to refuse the office and leave the parade to the top. Daniel had difficulty separating his Blackness from the knowledge that tthe person that he was writing the check to was anti-everything that stood for Black progress. Among his Black friends, Daniel frequently referred to the lobbyist as a blue-suit klansman.

Bowman went through some sort of metamorphosis during his term as treasurer and began to separate his Blackness from his responsibility as an officer of the association. He came to realize that in our society lobbying is often necessary to keep the legislative wheels from rolling over professional interests.

Another constant disturbance that plagued Bowman on his rise to the top was the lack of sensitivity and the openly negative attitudes toward minorities that were espoused by some of his peers. For example, Daniel's views about their mutual profession were usually accepted by his colleagues. But if he joined a conversation on economics, which is something that most people should have a winking knowledge about, they would interrupt him or plainly dismiss what he said by changing the subject.

Most white folks Bowman encountered seem to have a preconceived notion that economics is something that is a mystery to Black folks, while they strongly believe that Bowman is an authority on anything dealing with Black people. It is acceptable for Daniel to be knowledgeable about the works of Charles White and other Black artists, but he ignites mind bombs when he starts to discuss Bellini, Whistler or Rembrandt. Daniel was expected to know all about the jazz dance, but was never given a chance to reveal even a brushing acquaintance with the Highland fling, minuet or polka. He could talk at length about Walter Payton, Gale Sayers, Doug Williams and other Black football stars. He was sought after for information about L. Douglas Wilder, the governor of Virginia, and New York City Mayor David Dinkins. But he dare not be knowledgeable about Dwight D.

Eisenhower. White faces would seem to reflect: "What the hell do you know about Eisenhower? You're Black."

Daniel Bowman summarized some of his dealings with white folks in the organization:

> Most whites have some preconceived views about Blacks. And they don't want them disturbed. They are not comfortable turning loose the bias that their mother or father or somebody else in the family taught them. That's like being against the American flag and motherhood. So the easiest way for them to deal with you as a Black would be to keep that bias and make you an exception.
>
> Most Blacks in this country who have been around longer than two days have had some white folks say: 'You are not like the others. You're different. You are responsible.' The implication is that the rest of the Blacks are not. In other words, you're some sort of 'super nigger.'
>
> For example, years ago when Blacks were not permitted to participate in major league baseball, the reason whites gave for excluding them was that they didn't play the same caliber of baseball as the white boys. This, of course, was a bare-faced lie. Jackie Robinson, Larry Doby, Henry Thompson, Sam Jethroe, Sam Hairston, and the legendary Leroy "Satchel" Paige, and hundreds of other Black baseball greats had played major league baseball in the Negro National League (NNL) since the 1920s and in the Negro American League (NAL) since 1937.
>
> So what did they do when Branch Rickey brought Jackie Robinson along? It was easy for them to declare him an exception and classify him as a super second baseman. He was not an ordinary second baseman by any human measurement, so they could still keep their bias. He was a 'super nigger.'
>
> Yet, Blacks are called upon to accept mediocre or average white people every day. Blacks have been electing mediocre or just plain average white politicians since we first got the right to vote under the 15th Amendment in 1870. We have voted time and again for mediocre mayors. In contrast, if a Black mayor is elected, he's got to be a super mayor, not an ordinary mayor, not an average mayor, but a

super mayor. White America has different criteria when dealing with Black Americans. There are a lot of people in this country who are white-sheet racists to the bone and don't recognize it.

I recall the words of a white bus driver some years ago. The subject was open occupancy in housing. He said in a public meeting that I was chairing in a suburban community that he had no objections to Ralph Bunche's kids playing with his kids or even living next to him. Keep in mind Ralph Bunche won the Tappan prize for the best doctoral dissertation at Harvard in 1934. In 1950, he became the first Black person to be awarded the Nobel Peace Prize. In addition, he served as a United Nations undersecretary general for special political affairs from 1955 to October 1971, when he retired.

Yet, the bus driver had the audacity to think he was being liberal by offering to accept Dr. Bunche as his neighbor. His mindset was certainly no different from that of millions of other white Americans who feel that the color of their skin, washed or unwashed, gives them some God-given entitlement to superiority over any Black person, no matter how accomplished.

Although Daniel Bowman accomplished a great deal, he was most uncomfortable as president of a white trade association when social interaction was involved. Daniel is an excellent golfer who shoots consistently in the low 70s. As president of the association he was invited to play golf at a number of exclusive country clubs by various members of the association. However, because his color excluded him from membership in any of the clubs in his area, he could not reciprocate their invitations. Daniel felt that it would have been a personal put down for him to invite a colleague to join him on a public course, the only links accessible to him.

Membership in a country club certainly would have been appropriate for a person such as Daniel Bowman, who rose to the top of his professional organization. Not belonging to a country club is as much of a handicap to Bowman as to anyone who occupies executive suites of corporate America. How can Blacks think they've won equality if they can't operate from the same social level as their peers? Country clubs are as much a part of corporate America as the board room. It is on the patios and greens and in the bars of private clubs that many extended board meetings take place. Dan made the following observations on being excluded from the social order:

> There are different stratas or levels of communications between whites and Blacks. I have sometimes noted that even though people were calling me Dan, or whatever, and trying to assure me that they really were my good friends, they were always setting parameters. They would kiss my wife and I kissed theirs as a signal of a friendship, but we were excluded from the most personal conversations that people share with their close friends. Sometimes I would pick up bits of information that fell through the cracks from a white staff member. I realized before too much time passed that I could only get so close to my white colleagues. Those whites who really thought that they liked me locked me out and placed me in a category of people they accepted only in certain social or professional situations.

The minds of men and women are locked in early in their lives by their environment. Anything or anyone outside of that milieu is alien. Blacks in America have historically been treated as foreigners whose badge of disgrace is the color of their skin. Books have declared in bold type that being Black is a sin and loving Black is sinister. Nothing will change that prejudice until we are made to understand that skin tone is just that and does not negate the fact that Blacks are part of the human race. Nothing separates us but manmade circumstances. The irony in our history is that barriers like the Berlin Wall have been removed before Americans chose to knock down the barriers to racial equality.

THE CURSE OF BEING LIGHT,
BLACK AND BRIGHT

Jason Durham was born at the Harlem Hospital in New York City, December 25, 1922, during the apex of the Harlem Renaissance. His parents were physicians who owned a Stanford White-designed, turn-of-the-century Italiante residence on West 139th Street. Their neighborhood, the tree-lined blocks of 138th and 139th streets between Seventh and Eighth avenues, was populated by upward mobile Black residents who cultivated the lifestyle of the white millionaire home-owners who fled the area in 1919 when Negroes began to move to Sugar Hill in Uptown Manhattan. Their neighborhood was known locally as Strivers Row, a nickname bestowed by less fortunate Harlemites.

Madame C.J. Walker, America's first Black millionnairess and her daughter, A'Lelia; Dr. Louis T. Wright; musician Noble Sissle; orchestra leader Fletcher Henderson; and many other light-skinned families lived in the neighborhood. Strivers Row was also the home of a few dark-skinned brothers such as heavyweight boxer Harry Wills, comedian Stepin Fetchit and pianist-composer Eubie Blake. The Rev. Adam Clayton Powell Sr.'s family lived on the border of Strivers Row at 227 W. 136th St.

Although the Cotton Club was only a stone's throw from Strivers

Row, at 142nd and Lenox Avenue, Negroes were not admitted as guests to the internationally known entertainment mecca. Ironically, all of the entertainers, waiters, busboys, cooks and janitors were colored. Owney Madden's Cotton Club, although located in the heart of the Black ghetto, became the best-known entertainment plantation in America via radio broadcasts featuring such stars as Duke Ellington, Cab Calloway, Lucky Millinder, Louis Armstrong, Jimmy Lunceford, Ethel Waters, Lena Horne and Bill "Bojangles" Robinson.

The Durham family lived very comfortable on Strivers Row. Jason, the youngest of the three boys, was noticeably bright intellectually and in skin tone. Black students at Public School 5 frequently beat up the hazel-eyed blond because they thought he was Irish. On the other hand, when Jason crossed Eighth Street on the way to school or the grocery store, the Irish kids would jump him because they knew he was not one of them. Jason felt like he had been cursed because he was too light to be physically Black and genetically, by blood type according to the white establishment, too Black to be white.

In spite of Jason's mental confusion about his complexion, he was a star student in that he skipped every other grade and graduated from P.S. 5 when he was 11 years old. The young lad maintained a straight A average throughout his elementary school career. Thus, he was accepted at Townsend Harris Preparatory School for the College of the City of New York. The prep school, which was free for New York resident, had tough entry and academic standards. However, Jason was able to complete the four-year prep school curriculum within two years.

After graduation, his parents enrolled him in the Massachusetts Institute of Technology ((MIT) as a math major and a chemistry minor. At age 20, he had completed the necessary work to receive his baccalaureate, master's and doctorate degrees. Upon receiving his doctorate, he went to the Institute for Advance Study in Princeton, N.J. to continue his studies in mathematics. His academic work was interrupted in the fall of 1942 by World War II, at which time he accepted an assignment teaching mathematics and chemistry to soldiers who were being prepared for ordinance work at Aberdeen Proving Ground, Maryland.

In 1946, following the war, Jason took a job with an industrial company in Wilmington, Del. Durham made the following observations of how and why he took an industrial job as opposed to one in academia:

Most Ph.D. mathematicians in those days almost automatically gravitated to the best universities. I applied for a teaching or research post at 36 universities and learned that Black institutions of higher learning generally offered me a higher salary than the white universities. And there were a large number of white universities that declined to offer me anything at all. I want to emphasize that they were not saying, 'Well, we have applicants who are better qualified.' Some were more explicit. The University of Michigan people told me straight out, eyeball to eyeball, 'We don't think you would be comfortable in this environment. And we don't think our students would be comfortable with you.'

Although I was denied appointments at white universities because I was Black, I never gave a great deal of thought to passing for white. The people at MIT and other universities where I applied certainly knew that I was Black. There was never any question about my race.

However, my race wasn't that obvious to people in the private sector, who paid less attention to references and university transcripts.

The man who interviewed me at the Wilmington, Del., plant, who later became my boss, was a very refined gentleman. After I completed the interview, I had a letter in hand offering me a job. Mr. Rubenstein drove me to the train station at the end of the day. Before I got out of his car, he said, 'There's something I probably should talk to you about.' He told me that he was aware that I was a Negro and that he hoped that I would not let his knowledge of that fact affect my decision about accepting the position.

Then he told me something very interesting. He said that he had told several senior officers that he had learned from my records at MIT that I was Black. One of his bosses said to him something I have never forgotten: 'I am sorry you told me that. Because it is now impossible for me to judge this man on his merits. You should have simply told me he was a good guy, that you liked his record and his personality. But now you're the one who has raised the race question.'

The person who made that statement was a Jewish man

who knew first-hand some of the problems that minority groups face. We later became very good friends and I'm not sure to this day whether he's aware that I know he made those remarks. I never said one word to him about it.

I stayed in Wilmington for four years, married my childhood sweetheart and became the father of two children. During that time, the company had a high turnover in management. My new boss was considerably less interested in my well-being. My first boss was solicitous and always asked about my wife and children. He was candid and fair during my performance reviews. He patiently explained why I couldn't get more money and I never felt with him that I was being put upon or abused.

My next boss was the flip side of the coin. He wasn't necessarily a racist—I could have been white and he could have been just as indifferent to me and my work. I decided to confront him: 'Well, if I stay here, how much money will I make?'

When he answered, 'You might go up as much as 25 percent during the balance of your career,' I knew it was time to seek employment elsewhere.

I didn't have much difficulty getting a couple of good offers, one that included a starting salary of 25 percent more than I was making.

Durham accepted a position with the Pittsburgh firm that offered a 25 percent increase as opposed to the other offer of 30 percent more than his salary because he felt that there was more potential for growth. The Durhams moved to the all-white Squirrel Hill District in Pittsburgh, and Jason found his new position of manager of research and development was even better than he expected. He supervised about a hundred people, 99 percent of whom were white, many with Ph.D.s.

The Durham family blended perfectly with the residents of the Squirrel Hill community. Jason's wife Susan and their children had lighter skin tones than most of their Jewish neighbors, who assumed that the Durham family was White Anglo Saxon Protestant.

The community tranquility changed abruptly when Jason's father died and his obituary appeared in major newspapers across the nation. The Black cat was suddenly out of the bag. Jason described what followed:

We were caught by surprise by my father's sudden death. To our knowledge, he had never been seriously ill. Dad's passing and our unmasking as Negroes created more discontinuity in my wife's and children's lives than mine. My wife Susan noticed the change in attitudes of some of the people she came in touch with almost immediately. I didn't because I was sort of insulated. I spent most of my time at work. Some of the people at the company had known me at MIT, and knew I was Black. Susan, who had never been invited to join any of the social clubs anyway, observed an increased coolness from the neighbors. The children noticed it, too. Our daughter overheard snide racist remarks at school. Some of our son's former friends actually called him a nigger.

Susan was upset because she felt that she should have prepared our children to deal with racism, and we realized that we had to put a little more armor and a little more steel around them, as our parents had done for us.

My rationale was that the people who were looking for an excuse not to be friendly had their excuse now. We had many friends in the Black community. The fact that we lived in a predominantly white neighborhood was irrelevant. Susan was active with Alpha Kappa Alpha Sorority, and I was involved with Kappa Alpha Psi Fraternity. We frequently had Black guests in our home, and that was apparently alright with our neighbors. They just assumed that we were queer white folks.

About the same time that our social life in Pittsburgh became rocky, the company I was working for experienced a cash flow problem. I could see the financial handwriting on the wall and decided to look around again. By then, I had spent 10 years with the company and felt that I had made my contribution.

I was lucky. Word of my availability was on the grapevine just two weeks when I received an offer from a research company in San Diego, Calif. These people knew exactly who I was and what I was and there were no problems at all. They appointed me assistant chairman of the theoretical chemistry department and gave me a healthy boost over my previous salary. Though my title implied that

I had some management responsibilities, I really didn't have any. The chairman took care of most everything, and I filled in the gaps that he missed.

A problem surfaced about eight weeks after we moved to San Diego in 1966. I ran into some trouble in connection with race. It started when we attempted to buy a house. I didn't know much about San Diego but I found out there was a small but significant Black community in the southeast side of town. I can't call the Negro section a ghetto because it wasn't. It wasn't run down. It was more like some of the better Black communities in Los Angeles, Chicago, New York, Atlanta and Boston.

The company that I worked for was on the northwest side, about as far away as you could get geographically and sociologically. My wife and I decided we didn't want to live in the Black community because I didn't want to drive that far to work. So we bought a house in the section of San Diego called Lajala, a white upper middle class neighborhood. I offered the seller a little less than he was asking and he accepted it.

We were all set to move in when the stuff hit the fan. A senior vice president in our company sought out an official in one of the Lajala banks. 'Where is this guy getting his financing?' he asked. 'I want to stop it. I don't want him in Lajala.'

Of course, he couldn't stop me because I didn't need any financing. Green power is the best power. The seller had already signed the contract and couldn't back out of the deal. The broker was in the middle because she wanted her commission. So we closed the deal and moved in. We knew immediately that we were not welcome in the neighborhood. We would be sitting out in our backyard in the early evening and hear our neighbors to the left talking about how some people think they're as good as anybody. 'Don't they know they are not wanted? Why don't they leave?'

But we didn't 'just leave,' and those people eventually moved.

The neighbor on the right took a rather different attitude. 'I never thought I'd be living next to a Negro,' he said, 'but I am, and I don't see any difference from when I was living next to Nico (the guy from whom we purchased the house). So let's get on with life.' Our wives became reasonably good friends.

Susan became involved with the Episcopal church and our kids attended Sunday School. My wife worked with the guild and she was active in various church affairs. A church member invited us to a dance at a country club. When the vice president at the plant got wind of it he all but hit the ceiling. The invite meant we were going to go to his country club. He ranted to some of my associates that he didn't want any niggers in his club. Some of my friends advised me to pass up the invitation. They feared there would be trouble if I called his bluff. They also worried that I might be sorry because the results of my action might be something that I couldn't bring to a successful conclusion. They said, 'If you thumb your nose, he and his kind are gonna stomp on you, physically stomp you, not mentally harass you.'

So Susan and I had a long talk. I told her I didn't give a damn if I never go to another party, white, Black or polka dot. Putting on a tuxedo to go someplace is not my idea of fun. It never has been and never will be. My wife wanted to go in spite of the threat and we almost did. I'll never know what exactly would have happened, but I am certain it would have drawn battle lines in our company.

Rather than continue to work in a company where battle zones could be created overnight over racial trivia, Jason decided he would take a spin in academia. He accepted a professorship at a Black college on the assumption that he would be leaving the white and Black problem behind. He was wrong:

Initially, I was on sort of a roving assignment, working with three deans. I taught classes in chemistry, physics, mathematics and mechanical engineering. The faculty and the student bodies were mixed, and Black students were a small minority in the college of engineering. There was a significant number of white faculty. The chemistry faculty was rather interesting because it was not predominantly Black nor white; there was a significant number of Asians in the department.

In some situations, the Asians and Blacks would get
together and out-maneuver the whites. Sometimes the
whites and Asians would out-maneuver the Blacks. Those
coalitions would change and shuffle depending on the issues
involved. The chairman was Black but some of the white
professors had tenure and acted like chairmen, cutting deals
with the Black dean. Sometimes I wondered what the hell
was going on.

The animosity among these groups was real. Most of
the tenured professors in the physics department were
Jewish and I thought they would understand the problems
associated with being a minority. I think they did, but some
of them must have said, 'We'll do a little downtrodding
ourselves.'

I didn't automatically vote with the Black bloc. I would
listen to what the others had to say and sort of smooth
things out among the groups. I had no way of anticipating
or contemplating just what would come next.

After six years on the faculty, I took a sabbatical and
accepted an assignment working in an experimental
laboratory in Los Alamos, New Mexico. When I returned to
the university, the new dean refused to honor some of the
commitments that had been made by his predecessor. This
left me no option other than to terminate my services at the
institution.

My next move was to Salt Lake City, Utah, headquarters
of the Church of Jesus Christ of Latter-day Saints. Here I
found religion and racism being stirred in one pot. The city
was probably 60 to 70 percent Mormon. Don't let anybody
kid you. They run the place. The mayor was Mormon. All
city councilmen were Mormons. The members of the school
board were Mormons.

I've had Black employees at the company come to me
and say, 'I can't stay here. My kids are being called nigger in
school. When I go to the school to talk to the principal, the
principal refuses to even see me.' The general managers and
officers in our firm who were not Mormons learned how to
get along with them quick. Mormons in our organization
protected one another, although they treated women on a
lower level.

The official position of the Mormon church relegated Blacks to second-class citizenship. Blacks were not entitled to be full members in the Mormon church until relatively recently, within the last decade. I'll never forget the day when the president of our company said, 'I know now what it is like to be a minority. It doesn't matter whether you are white or Black. If you are not a Mormon here, you are dirt. You're either white dirt or Black dirt. It doesn't matter.'

The president and the vice president, who was my immediate supervisor, were fired because they couldn't resolve a serious personality conflict with several members of the board of directors. I was now in the number one position to become president according to the organizational chart. They scraped that chart and picked a white boy. Could it have been called racism? Could it have been a statement that most corporate executives in Salt Lake City were not ready to have a Black guy as the president and chief executive officer of their companies?

Could it have been age discrimination? The corporation had been going through some shuffles, bringing in some younger guys at the executive level, guys in their late 40s. The man they selected to replace my boss and to become my new boss was a man in his late 40s. A man who worked one level below me was promoted above me, so it could have been age. It could have been that some people sincerely felt that Durham didn't have what it took to do the job. They never told me.

I am still upset and annoyed by the fact that they didn't even discuss it. They just came into my office one day and announced: 'Frank Blank is the new president. I hope you will find it possible to work with him.' I replied that I had known the young fellow and considered him bright and capable and saw no reason why I couldn't work with him. But I said to myself, if there is a reason, we will find out. But in any case, my attitude hasn't changed. I think they should have offered me the position. I think that I could have handled it, and would have relished the opportunity. The young fellow could have had the presidency four years later when I reached the mandatory retirement age.

The new president was smooth in some respects, but he

never came down to talk to me about how he wanted to work with me. My former boss was the managerial type who needed someone with the technical credentials he didn't have. The new president did not need a deputy with my credentials. I could see that 10 miles away. I started thinking, 'It's time to go back to New York,' and six months later I did.

Jason Durham is a brilliant man whose most productive years have passed. The shame of it all is that America watched this genius go to waste because he was cursed with the number one sin in the United States, and that is being born Black.

America can no longer afford to waste its human resources as it has exploited its natural resources for more than a century. Our country must learn to heed the admonition of the United Negro College Fund: "A mind is a terrible thing to waste."

HOW CAN A BLACK MAN WIN IF TARZAN IS HIS HERO?

Wade Caldwell was born during the worst of times on September 26, 1930, in Indianapolis, Ind., when the Great Depression was beginning to wrap its cold arms around the American people. The Ku Klux Klan and their dogma were reigning supreme throughout the state. Every institution in Indiana outside of the Black ghettos was off-limits to colored people, including the churches and the gasoline station toilets. The train station waiting rooms were segregated into spaces labeled "for whites only," or "for colored only."

Wade, the second of Jethro and Rachel Mae Caldwell's three children, was born in a "for colored only" hospital ward. The Caldwell's first child, who died of pneumonia, was buried in a "for colored only" graveyard. Jethro was a 25-cents-per-hour laborer; Rachel worked part-time as a maid and cook in the homes of several depression-proof white families for $1.50-per-day.

The senior Caldwell had not received one stitch of formal education beyond the third grade, and that was acquired in a one-room unpainted schoolhouse in the backwoods near Gallion, Ala. Somewhere between Alabama and Indiana, Jethro learned to write his name in Old English script, which was commonly used on high school diplomas and college degrees in the 1920s and '30s.

Young Wade must have been greatly influenced by his father. He began scribbling his name in that style long before he entered elementary school. In addition to printing and writing like his dad, he made line drawings of anything that attracted his fancy. One of his greatest pleasures as a child was drawing caricatures, especially of the family preacher and of the ladies who wore fancy hats, while he sat in the children's section of the church on Sunday mornings.

Although Wade received prizes and awards for art during his elementary school years, he did not take his drawing talents seriously until he reached his sophomore year at the for-colored-only Crispus Attucks High School in Indianapolis. His main goal until he reached age 15 was to become a big-time athlete. The idea of becoming an artist was not peaked by any grand plan—Wade had no formal art training—but by an incident that took place in a geometry class. Wade recalls:

I thought I was a big shot. I was the high school state and city champion of the high jump. I did not feel I had to put forth any sweat in geometry. I thought my sports status entitled me to an automatic pass. Paul Gore, the math instructor, decided he would bear down on me and teach me some humility in addition to some geometry. He gave me a lot of extra assignments to take home. I didn't like geometry so, of course I didn't like him. I was so disgusted with that man that one day in class I decided to draw a funny caricature of him. The more I worked on the drawing at my desk, the better it looked to me. The instructor was easy to draw because his ears and nose were oversized. My depiction was so good that I decided to pass it around to other members of the class. The drawing circulated from desk to desk and the kids were laughing but the teacher didn't know why.

Finally, a girl by the name of Ruby Lee Raymond got it. Since she was the teacher's pet, she gave him the drawing. Mr. Gore looked at it for only several seconds, but to me it seemed like hours.

'Okay, Wade,' Mr. Gore said, 'I want you to wait after class.' I thought my goose was cooked.

In those days, teachers whipped children who misbehaved, so I thought, here comes another whipping. But after class, Mr. Gore said, 'I want you to sign this picture.'

I thought to myself, this man must think I'm some kind of idiot if he thinks I am going to incriminate myself by signing my name. I refused: 'I'm not going to sign it.'

'I want you to autograph it,' he insisted.

I really thought he was playing with my intelligence and I blurted, 'I'm not gonna autograph it either.'

With a broad smile on his face, Mr. Gore said, 'Look Wade, I want to keep this picture. It's good. I want to frame it and put it on the wall in my den at home. There are people who make a pretty good living doing exactly what you have done.'

Then, he told me to sit down because he wanted to explain something to me. After a pause, he said, 'Wade, you are a very talented young artist and I think you should give serious thought to making drawing your career choice.' In retrospect, I can fully appreciate that Mr. Gore's encouragement made a very deep impression on me. He really put me on the road to becoming an editorial cartoonist.

Wrestling with the idea of becoming a great artist and a great athlete posed a dilemma for me as a teenager. To make matters worse, I was the state broad jumping champion the year I finished high school. My track coach, John E. Smith always thought of me as a strong, no-nonsense athlete. He arranged for me to visit the University of Illinois at Champaign/Urbana, his alma mater, to try out for the track team. I justified his faith in me by making the team.

Coach Smith was delighted when I became the Big 10 champion in the high jump in 1951 and the Big 10 broad jump champion in 1953. I've always maintained if you want to eat, you've got to jump. I eat well.

I was the hero on the track team, but I was a heel in the classroom. The art instructor would look at my work and say, 'Well, it doesn't grab me.'

'What does that mean, sir?' I would ask. 'It doesn't grab me,' he'd repeat without explaining what he meant.

Racism was rampant at the University of Illinois during that period, so I didn't know whether it was my work or my race that he was judging. I decided to put it to a test. I started signing my first name backward, E-D-A-W, on my drawings. We had to submit four finished works each semester for that class. Our work was entered in an exhibit that was judged by instructors in the art department. To my surprise, the entries signed Edaw won commendations while the ones bearing my own name drew grades of C. By the end of the semester, I had to acknowledge that I drew the pictures signed Edaw.

When my major professor found out, he was stunned. 'Oh no, this 'A' work couldn't be yours, Wade,' he protested.

'Oh, yes,' I said, 'It is my work.' Thank God it was too late for him to change the grade. I graduated from the U of I with a bachelor's degree in commercial art.

Too many white professors have preconceptions of a Black person's capabilities, almost from the moment they lay eyes on us. They make up their minds when you walk into a classroom that you are either a 'C' or a 'D' student, and that's what you're gonna get, with a few exceptions.

The same mentality carries over into corporate management. Most supervisors just assume that you are dumb and lax in your work, regardless to what you do. If you come in early, they'll feel you have some ulterior motive for doing so. If you stay late, you get the same kind of treatment. As a matter of fact, they might even ask you why you came in early or stayed late?

I was lucky with my first job after I graduated from college. The publisher who hired me was truly an All-American. He didn't have one ounce of bias in his body. He was a man who judged you by your talent rather than the color of your skin.

My co-workers, in their heart of hearts, were not biased either, but they definitely were patronizing. There were a couple of guys I worked with who wouldn't allow me to answer a question. For instance, if somebody walked up to me and said, 'Wade, how long have you been drawing editorial cartoons?' One of them would jump in and say, 'Oh, he's been at it a long time.'

Or a visitor might ask how long had I been drawing caricatures of politicians. Again one of my associates would interrupt: 'Oh, he's been doing this for years. He's great.'

They felt that they had to speak for me to validate my competence for those white people. They exhibited their bias indirectly by assuming I didn't have the intelligence to acquit myself in white circles.

There was no organized racism. They couldn't help speaking for me in general conversations like, 'Wade, where did you get your training?' That's a simple question but one of my colleagues would say, 'Oh, he went to the University of Illinois.'

These are the kinds of things that white folks feel that they have to do to give credibility to a Black man's talent, which is nonsense. After enduring this for a while, you become very sensitive, even over-sensitive.

Among the other humiliations found in the workplace are the ethnic jokes. If somebody springs a Polish joke on you, you can bet the next joke to jump out of the box will be a Black joke.

You can always tell when a racist joke is about to surface. They always ask, 'Would you be offended if I told you a joke?' You don't want to appear to be thin-skinned, so you say, 'Let's hear it.'

The joke invariably begins, 'These two Black guys were walking down the street . . .' I found myself preparing white jokes just to protect myself.

If I could laugh at their jokes, then they could laugh at mine. But they dropped those jokes in my presence pretty soon after I adopted the role of jester.

Another time that they rub salt in your wounds is during coffee and lunch breaks. Somebody will usually relate crime they read or heard about. 'Did you read about this Black guy who committed (murder or rape)? Wade, did you know him?'

Obviously I never knew any of those people.

I finally developed a defense for this kind of situation in order to keep my self-respect. I searched for incidents where white folks had done something wrong. I even went so far as to have my wife cut out articles about white folks' crimes. That was the only way I could keep my sanity. You almost become overprotective of your turf.

When Richard Speck did his thing, I saved all the

articles. When the story broke, I took the articles to work with me. I could hardly wait for the coffee break to spring my revenge.

I did not get a direct response, but the crime story telling soon stopped.

I'm sure other Blacks in management suffer similar incidents but handle them in their own way.

There was another Black guy at our newspaper who was high up in the eschelon of management. Everytime you saw him, he was laughing. There might be nothing funny, but you could hear him laughing his ass off when talking with his white counterparts. It wasn't normal, but it was his defense mechanism.

On several occasions I would talk to this guy and he would keep up that happy facade, telling me about the great opportunities he had in moving up in management. But I'm sure that somewhere in the back of his head he felt that he would never really get to the top. That's devastating when you have the capability.

The strain finally took its toll on this fellow in November 1989, when he had a stroke, and in early 1990, when he had a triple bypass.

Another common put down I've encountered is from white secretaries who would actually ask me if I carried a knife. And they were sincere. Others would say, 'I had some nice colored fellow cutting my grass the other day, and do you know he didn't steal anything.' What she was really saying was that all Blacks are not thieves.

Unfortunately, there are a lot of people running loose around this country who harbor all kinds of negative ideas about Black people, regardless of who we are, where we are or how much training or education we have. You can throw your degrees at them, but it doesn't matter. They cling to their misconceptions.

I'm surprised that some psychiatrists or psychologists don't classify racism as a mental illness. I think if it was treated as such, it would go a long way toward solving a real serious problem. But first one must realize that you are crazy before you can go about the business of uncrazing yourself.

Black management people jump through crazy hoops every day, whether they admit it or not. They're all sitting on a hot seat. I don't care how big a big shot a Black guy may be sitting at General Motors or some other Fortune 500 company, smoking a cigar with the rest of the boys, he is catching hell. He likely will burn out because he is continually jumping through crazy hoops. He can't divorce himself from being Black because they won't allow him to. Sometimes he wishes, 'God, I wish I could just blend in and don't stand out so much.'

And there is another type of manager. I call him the enforcer. He is an enforcer for all the corporate problems. He leans over backward to prove to the executives that he's not partial toward Blacks because he is Black. This kind of Negro will chop up a Black for breakfast and eat him to prove his fairness. He is making a point to his superiors: 'Watch my actions, race means nothing to me.'

Let me give you another example of something that happened to me. I was involved in creating an animated cartoon production for a major oil company that had allocated a large sum of money for Black involvement. I charged $65,000, which was a bargain-basement price, to produce a 10-minute television segment encouraging minority participation in their affirmative action program.

I was asked to meet with six of the company's top executives. After I made my presentation, they looked at one another and nodded approval. 'This is all right. This is great,' one of them enthused. 'I think we can go with this.'

However, the acting chairman of the meeting said, 'Before we can sign off on this, we must show it to our minority management officer.' So he pushed a button and this handsome, clean-cut Black guy walked in, sharp as a tack.

The man looked around at everybody in the room. All the whites were looking at him. He was trying to get a signal from them, but he didn't get one. Finally he said, 'I don't like it.' Then the acting chair said, 'Okay, if he doesn't like it, then we can't approve it.'

This guy knocked me out of the box and knocked me out of an opportunity to make $65,000 from a company that might have given me more assignments. He obviously followed the old adage, if in doubt, punt. He was conditioned to respond a certain way and he did.

To this day I maintain it was partly my fault. I should have given him the signal, but I didn't. I should have said, 'Everybody likes my work, but they wanted your approval.'

Black folks, like other Americans, can be conditioned and brainwashed by newspapers, magazines, books, movies, television and radio.

When I was a youngster, Tarzan the Ape Man was my favorite hero. My friends and I would go junking in those days, picking up Coke and milk bottles in the alleys and turning them into the stores for a penny a piece. If we worked hard, we could accumulate enough to go to the Saturday matinee, which cost a dime. We went to the neighborhood theater every week to see the latest episode of that Edgar Rice Burrough character, Tarzan.

In each serial, there would always be a scene where beautiful Jane, who was played by Maureen O'Sullivan, would have been captured by a tribe of African natives. They would tie her to a big tree, and do a war dance around her while beating jungle drums. We kids would sit on the edge of our seats, hoping and praying that Tarzan (Johnny Weismueller) would come and save her.

Just as the suspense reached a climax that was almost unbearable, we would hear this wild animalistic cry. The cameras would then focus on the tallest tree in the jungle, and there would stand Tarzan, a big half-naked white man with a butcher knife in his mouth. He would swing through the trees like a monkey, coming to save Jane. We kids would holler and scream, 'Get 'em Tarzan, go get 'em.'

One of my friends would become so overwhelmed by what was going on on the movie screen that he actually turned flips of joy in the aisle of the theater. Some big boys threw their hats in the air when Tarzan rescued Jane. I said, 'God, Tarzan was a great guy.'

Wow! The biggest fight I ever got into in my life was about Tarzan. It started over who was gonna play Tarzan and who was gonna be one of the natives. I knew damn well I didn't want to play a native because all of the natives were short, pot-bellied Black guys with no muscles. Whereas, Tarzan was a strapping muscular man and, I was determined to be Tarzan. Subliminally, the movie had taken over my brain and I was aware of little other than the fact that I didn't want to be a Black native. It did not occur to me that I was Black and Tarzan and Jane were white. I fought for the honor to play Tarzan and I won.

I got into another fight over Tarzan when I bet several of my little friends that Tarzan could beat Joe Louis. I knew Joe Louis was good, but I thought Tarzan was better. It never occurred to me that Tarzan was fiction. Both Tarzan and Joe Louis were real flesh and blood to us in those days.

One afternoon, Tarzan almost got me killed. I was being chased by a gang of half-pint hoodlums when I remembered Tarzan had a trick that he always pulled. When the natives pursued Tarzan, he would suddenly stop and fall on his hands and knees in front of them. The dumb natives would just keep running and fall over his back. Tarzan then would spring up and escape in the opposite direction. I thought this was very clever.

I tried the same trick on the sidewalks of Indianapolis. I was tired and the half-pint hoodlums were on my heels. I said, 'What the hell would my hero do under these circumstances? He'd fall on his hands and knees and they'd fall over his back.' I fell on my hands and knees and discovered that I had made a big mistake. They did not run over me. They jumped on me and beat me every place except the bottom of my feet.

When I recovered, I muttered, 'Damn, something's wrong. Tarzan has been pulling my leg. Indianapolis is not Hollywood. And Hollywood is not real life.' Never in life will I fall on my hands and knees again.

Unfortunately, the media is so strong that most people go to their graves without ever realizing the difference between Hollywood and life in the real world.

FROM KINDERGARTEN TO THE PRESIDENCY OF CHICAGO'S LARGEST CORPORATE EMPLOYER, THE PUBLIC SCHOOL SYSTEM

Frank W. Gardner was born June 12, 1923, at St. Luke's Hospital, 14th Street and Michigan Avenue in Chicago during the period when Black people could enter and leave the hospital in only one way: through the back door located on the Indiana Avenue side of the institution.

Frank W. was the first of two sons of Frank Jr. and Eva Gardner. Eva, a native Chicagoan, graduated from the Sherwood Elementary School and Frank Jr., who migrated to Chicago from Bessemer, Ala., in 1917, never completed his primary education. The Gardners instilled strict discipline and a thirst for academic excellence in Frank and Edward.

The elder Gardner's first job in Chicago was as a laborer at Karpen's Furniture Factory. In 1919, he gained employment as a handyman at the U.S. Customs House on South Canal. Frank's drive and ambition resulted in a promotion to electrician's helper. The industrious Mr. Gardner became a bonafide civil service electrician. By the early 1930's, the Gardners were able to contract with Sears, Roebuck and Company to build their home at 9140 S. Michigan.

Frank Jr.'s highest ambition was to see his sons in government positions that would provide them security and a decent living. He envisioned Frank and Edward working at the main post office, where he knew they would receive regular paychecks and the social status and prestige post office employment provided during the 1930s, '40s and '50s. Blacks working in the post office during those years were on an economic level with many Black physicians and lawyers, some of whom worked there full time and practiced medicine and law part time. Frank Gardner Jr. never envisioned the degree of success his sons actually attained. The father did not live to see Edward become one of the wealthiest men in America or Frank at the pinnacle of power at the Chicago Board of Education.

After graduating from Gillespie Elementary School, which had a 100 percent Black student population, young Frank entered Fenger High School, where there were only 10 Blacks among 1,500 students. Frank W. did extremely well academically at Fenger, graduating as an honor student, but he caught hell on the football field. In a practice game with Lane Tech, Frank's teammates taunted him unmercifully: "Get the nigger, get the nigger." He didn't know which side to run from and was hit from all sides. They kicked him, elbowed him, tripped him and stepped on his fingers. Coach Chuck Palmer removed Frank from the team for his own good.

Frank W. enrolled in the Chicago Teachers College in 1942. His education was interrupted by World War II in 1943, when he volunteered to serve in the U.S. Army. Gardner was honorably discharged as a staff sergeant in 1946, re-entered the Chicago Teachers College and graduated in 1948 with a B.A. degree. His grades were so high in mathematics that a white female student sought to copy from his homework papers and tests. She stayed as close to him as wallpaper throughout his junior and senior years. At Chicago Teacher's, it was the custom for students who walked down the aisles together at graduation to hold hands. When Frank extended his hand to his copy-cat classmate during rehearsal, she recoiled. Frank was hurt but not depressed by the reaction of the young woman who had used him as though he were a paper towel to be discarded.

In keeping with their father's dictum, Frank W. and Edward began their careers not at the post office but as teachers in one of the largest school systems in the nation, the Chicago public schools.

Frank remembers his first experience as a teacher:

Moments after I walked into Jenner Elementary School,
located at 1009 N. Cleveland Avenue near Cabrini-Green, I
was nonplused by the expression on the face of a white male

teacher who stood with some other teachers in the hall near
the main entrance. As I passed by, he scowled at me and
remarked, 'Here's another one.'

I swallowed my pride and kept moving because I didn't
want to do anything that would mar my record the first day
on job.

The Jenner faculty was predominantly white in those
days. There were only three of us Negroes in the entire
school. There wasn't even a Black janitor. Even the smoke
coming out of the chimney was white.

Most of the white teachers were as cordial as one might
expect considering that they had only worked with a few
Black teachers during their career, but several were
downright rude and nasty.

At the end of the semester, I started work at the
Dennison Company handling paper boxes. Although I had a
college degree, work in the warehouse was the best summer
job I could find. After two days of working along side of
white kids who had not even finished high school, I said this
does not make sense. I just dropped my work apron on the
floor and walked away. I immediately enrolled in graduate
school at DePaul University.

When I returned to Jenner Elementary that September,
I requested a transfer to the Gillespie Elementary School at
9301 S. State, a school I had graduated from 13 years earlier.
Eileen Stack, the principal at Gillespie, gave me a great deal
of encouragement and said she was impressed with my
work. Her successor, Thelma Gray, a Black woman, also
appreciated my work with the kids and their parents. She
offered me an opportunity to become head teacher at the
Drew School, a branch of Gillespie, in Princeton Park, just a
few blocks west of State Street, off of 95th Street. The grade
levels at Drew were kindergarten through third grade.

While I was at Drew School, I was brought to the
attention of Anna Koleheim, a very brilliant Black educator.
Ms. Koleheim, the principal of Betsy Ross Elementary
School, 6059 S. Wabash Ave., offered me the opportunity to
work with her as the assistant principal at Betsy Ross.

I consulted with Ms. Gray, who said she thought it was a
great opportunity because there were no administrative

vacancies at Gillespie. I thought I was making pretty good progress by becoming an assistant principal only six years after entering the school system.

While I was the assistant principal at Betsy Ross, I took the principal's exam and failed. I couldn't understand how I failed the exam because I had studied very hard for it. But I failed it. The second time that I took it, about a year later, I passed the written part with flying colors. Some of my peers warned me that the oral part of the exam was very tough. I took the oral with no difficulty because I had had a lot of on-the-job experience. I was very knowledgeable about school administration because Ms. Koleheim had given me free reign as assistant principal at Betsy Ross.

After passing the principal's exam I was placed on a list with approximately 67 other people, six of whom were Black. At that time, Blacks were assigned only to Black schools, while whites could be placed in any of the 600 schools in the Chicago system. I decided that waiting for an opening in a Black school was nonsense. I was aware of a vacancy in Hyde Park at the William A. Ray Elementary School, 5631 S. Kimbark, and arranged for a meeting with Dr. Chris Melnick, the district superintendent. During our talk, Dr. Melnick surprised me by saying, 'You sound like you're interviewing me.' I asked him to explain. 'You know all the right questions to ask,' he responded. 'Your questions indicate that you know something about the business of running a school.'

I informed him that I had been an assistant principal for approximately 10 years during which time Principal Koleheim had allowed me unbridled freedom to delve into the rudiments of school administration, policy making and other elements of running a school day by day.

Dr. Melnick said, 'The Ray School is one of the toughest schools in the system, very high on the scale academically. The community will eat you up alive.'

I retorted that I didn't think that would happen.

'The principal who just left was figuratively torn apart,' Dr. Melnick said. 'That's why she left. The one who preceded her suffered the same fate. Principals don't last at Ray School very long. And remember, Ray School has never had a Black principal. The school is predominantly white.'

I told the superintendent I didn't care if the Ray School was populated with purple people. I wanted to become the principal of that school.

'Where are you on the list?' he asked. I said my name was at the top, that I was next in line for a principalship. I knew that the school system had historically followed a policy of waiting until a cluster of schools became available, appointing Black administrators to the Black schools and leaving the predominantly white schools such as Ray for white administrators.

Dr. Melnick was convinced that Gardner would be an asset to Ray School, and acquainted Benjamin Willis, the general superintendent of schools, with Gardner's qualifications. Willis added his blessings to Melnick's recommendation and Frank Gardner was appointed the principal at Ray School.

Seymour Banks, president of Ray's parent-teacher association, sent the new principal a welcoming letter dated August 26, 1965:

Dear Mr. Gardner:

As president of the Ray School PTA, I'd like to extend a welcome to you and congratulate you upon your appointment as principal. We would be delighted to do all in our power to help you in your new assignment and acquaint you with the neighborhood.

If you'd like to get together for a chat, either formally or informally, please call me either at my home or at my office.

Last spring we set up a program for the 1965-1966 school year without knowing anything about the change in principals. Our plans call for Mrs. Knous to speak to the PTA at the first meeting and at a dinner followed by a talk by an outside speaker at the October meeting. Obviously we would like to meet you as early as possible and have you address our PTA, but we quite understand that a principal coming to a new school may be quite busy for a while.

We would appreciate it a great deal if you would call either me or our program chairman, Mrs. Eileen Gengewirth, to discuss some date at which it would be convenient for you to speak to our general meeting. Once more, welcome to Ray.

Sincerely,

Seymour Banks
President, Ray PTA

Gardner recalls his delight over their acceptance:

It was a great experience. The Ray School was an outstanding example of school-based management. I have been in communication with the activities of Ray School. I have received copies of their school calendar. They didn't have to do that. Ray School was granted $50,000 in addition to their budget by a community organization called Friends of Ray School. This money was used at the principal's discretion. Some of the funds were used by the music department, the library, some went toward the purchase of computers and other equipment. Other groups paid for ancillary needs such as new drapes, a Great Books program and a music enrichment program. Very few schools in Chicago had benefits and resources like those at the Ray School.

Gardner said that Ray School also benefited from its proximity to the University of Chicago. Frank was instrumental in establishing a very productive cooperative program, and his contributions did not go unnoticed. Gardner received a letter from the University of Chicago Graduate School of Education dated June 8, 1967:

Dear Mr. Gardner:

May I take this inappropriate means of expressing my appreciation to you for your cooperation this year with our elementary school education program. It should go without saying that the classroom experience our students had have better equipped them to enter the teaching profession.

Unfortunately, the only way the extra time and effort
toward this program created for you and your staff can be
replaced is by this short note of thanks. But I suppose the
ultimate reward for all of us is in knowing that, for the most
part, we have had a hand in contributing to elementary
education a small number of dedicated and promising young
teachers.

Again my thanks for your part in the program and my best
wishes for the summer.

Cordially,

Richard E. Hodges
Director, Elementary Teachers Education Program

Frank asked:

How is a West or South Side ghetto school going to
compete with Ray with that kind of support? Keep in mind
that these parents were middle-class, some upper-middle
class and some were wealthy. Parents from all these
communities actively participate in the school programs. On
the other side of the coin, I've seen a few cases of better
teaching at Jenner and Betsy Ross, the so-called ghetto
schools, than I saw at Ray. It is the support system at Ray
School that enables bright youngsters to score high both
locally and nationally, in every area tested. The principal
and the teachers received the credit, but it was the resources
available at Ray School that really made the difference.
   Imbalance of resources frightens me. I think school-
based management has tremendous possibilities but I'm
concerned about the equity. For instance, the Ray people
write proposals for federal and other grants with the
assistance of the University of Chicago people, who are all
pros at this game. It's a no-lose situation for the students at
Ray School.

On January 17, 1968, the *Hyde Park Herald* reported:

Federal funds are being sought to establish an independent learning center at the William H. Ray School.

St. Thomas the Apostle School and the University of Chicago Laboratory School will cooperate in the project, which will be financed under Title III of the Elementary and Secondary Education Act of 1965.

Officially, the application was submitted by the Chicago Board of Education. But actually it was conceived and prepared by Principal Frank Gardner and a group of Ray parents.

In the application, Ray is described as an integrated public school, serving children of a wide socioeconomic range and a wide diversity of educational needs.

Frank's role in the Title III project was acclaimed by the Ray School PTA, as evidenced in a letter of January 11, 1968:

Dear Mr. Gardner:

We are overjoyed to hear that the Ray School Title III proposal has been accepted by the U.S. Office of Education and the Board of Education as part of a Chicago comprehensive project.

On behalf of our PTA, I want to thank you for the fine leadership you've exhibited as principal of Ray in bringing the learning center project to fruition. Without your tenure in our school, with its emphasis on changing our school into a true community school, reflecting a real cooperation and trust between the administration and parents, even thinking of such projects would have been impossible. Since you've left our school, your continued interest in this project has been most helpful in many ways.

I think you should write a "how-to" article on transferring a four-wall school into a community school. Your success has made you imminently qualified to do so.

I hope your Title III project will be the first of many such
good experiences at Ray School.

Sincerely,

Jean M. Solomon (Mrs. Robert S. Solomon)
President, Ray School PTA

Gardner observed:

Whitney Young High School, at 211 S. Laflin, is a good
example of a school that accepts students from all over the
city of Chicago. Whitney Young does not have a district.
The entire city is its district. Whitney Young has the choice
of accepting youngsters from any place in the city provided
the students can pass the entrance exam. Whitney Young is
selective, but schools like Kenwood High are not. Kenwood
is selective only to the degree that they have vacant seats.
They must take everyone in their district.
     Beasley Elementary at 5255 S. State St., is another
school with a lot of goodies. Selective students. Selective
staff. Magnet schools such as Beasley are designed to keep
non-minorities in the Chicago Public School system, and it
works. Middle-class students are actually bused to the school
located in the front yard of the Robert Taylor projects.
These kids come from all over the city to the Beasley School
because of the excellent academic program that it offers.
Some families are actually pulling youngsters out of private
schools and sending them to magnet schools like Beasley,
LaSalle Language Academy at 1734 N. Orleans St., and Walt
Disney, 4140 N. Marine Dr. Our magnet elementary schools
are in the same class as the Whitney Youngs, Lanes and
Lindbloms. What you really have in those kinds of schools is
a private school operation in a public school system.
     In early winter 1968, I received a call from James
Redmond, the general superintendent of the Chicago public
schools. 'Frank, why don't you come down and talk to me
for a while?' he suggested. 'Can you make it? Do you have
time to come down Thursday afternoon and see me?' I had
never talked to Superintendent Redmond in my life, but he

was so cordial that he made me feel like an old friend. Of course I agreed to a meeting.

I visited with Dr. Redmond at his office in the Chicago Board of Education headquarters, 228 N. LaSalle.

After exchanging pleasantries, he said, 'Frank, we're going to have a vacancy on the board of examiners, an organization set up by state statute to be responsible for certifying and licensing all principals and teachers in the Chicago School System. Bill Reich is the person who is holding that position now and he's going to retire. They've never had a Black on the board. I'm going to create a temporary position over there for you. I want you there. I'm going to call it assistant to the board of examiners. I want you to work there and become familiar with the job.'

Frank received a confirmation of his impending promotion in a letter of February 14, 1968:

Dear Mr. Gardner:

The Board of Education, at its meeting today, approved my recommendations for your transfer and appointment to the position of assistant to the Board of Examiners, effective March 1, 1968.

Your fine background of experience as a teacher to the principalship of Ray Elementary School provides evidence of your ability to accept the challenges and responsibilities of the position.

Please accept my congratulations and best wishes upon your appointment. I am confident that you will find your new role to be interesting and stimulating.

Sincerely,

James F. Redmond
General Superintendent of Schools

Frank continued:

I felt good about the appointment. Here's another
promotion, and an opportunity to go downtown. A week
later, I reported to Bill Reich, who happened to have been
my high school counselor at Fenger High School. I told him
I was sent over there by Dr. Redmond to be the assistant to
the board of examiners. His jaw dropped six inches. His
disappointment was evidenced by the kind of work he
assigned me. For the next six months, I folded boxes and
patted papers and worked in the storeroom. It was
demeaning. I took it only because I had an ace in the hole,
Superintendent Redmond. I knew this was for only a matter
of time.

Bill Reich made sure that I spent the next six months in
hell. But I was determined to bear it out because I knew
what was coming. Otherwise, I couldn't have taken his
treatment. Reich obviously had some other person in mind
to replace him.

Bill Reich, in my opinion, was a bigot. I watched him
operate from afar and saw how he treated Black applicants
when they came into his office. It was just so belittling.

I remember a very tall and handsome Black man applied
for a position in the field of physical education. Reich patted
him on the back and gave him all kinds of verbal
encouragement, though he had no intention of hiring the
young man. He even told the applicant, 'You look like just
the kind of gym teacher we need,' but the young man didn't
have a snowball's chance in hell of getting that job.

One day Dr. Redmond called both Reich and me into his
office. He said, 'Bill, you know Frank of course. He's going
to be your successor.' Bill flopped down in his chair. His face
became ashen. He looked like death eating a soda cracker.
He just couldn't believe it. He couldn't fathom how
Superintendent Redmond was going to put a Black man in a
post where he would be making decisions that affect the
entire school system.

Finally, when Reich departed shortly before the
Christmas holidays in 1968, I became a member of the board
of examiners.

There are only three members on the board: chairman,
vice chairman and secretary. I was the secretary; Dr. Morton

Elenbogen was vice chairman and Dr. James Redmond was the chairman. We each had a single vote. Dr. Elenbogen and I pretty much voted together on all issues.

Before I served on the board of examiners, there had been fewer than 20 Black principals in the history of the Chicago school system. The first principal's examination that I helped administer was offered to our system through the Educational Testing Service in Princeton, N.J. Seventy-five Blacks passed that principal's exam.

I asked myself, 'Did we suddenly get smart?' I don't know how it happened because we had had so few Black administrators through the years and all of a sudden on one examination, 75 Blacks passed.

Grades on such tests are coded. You're a number, not a name. When we started matching names and numbers, I was astonished to see so many Black names coming up. I said, 'My God! All these Blacks are passing.' I couldn't believe it. Then I thought maybe it was a freak but fortunate accident.

When the principal's examination was given four years later, I was still on the board and another near-miracle occurred: More than half of the people who passed the new examination were Black. Success seems to have bred success.

Chicago Blacks became more test-wise and gained higher marks on the principal's exam about the same time that a desegregation decree came down from Washington indicating that the board could no longer discriminate between Black and white principals in school assignments. Chicago was ordered to integrate the administration as well as the faculty. And we did it. We also integrated the counseling staff.

My work as a member of the board of examiners went very well until one morning when Joseph Hannon, the new general superintendent of the schools, called me into his office and said, 'You know, the people in Hyde Park are dissatisfied with the situation over there. I suppose you know they are demanding that I send you to District 14.'

I didn't know what he was talking about. I had no idea. He said, 'The University of Chicago people and the Hyde Park people want you.' They had transferred Donald Blythe,

the former district superintendent, to the central office
downtown.

So the next thing I knew, I got marching orders to
report to the district superintendent's office at Hyde Park
High School, 6220 S. Stony Island.

My coming aboard as the new district superintendent
made headlines in the *Hyde Park Herald* newspaper.
Among other things, the article said that 'assigning Mr.
Gardner to the district superintendent seat was like icing on
the cake.' The article was filled with accolades.

Hyde Park High School was my initial headquarters, but
we were moved to Kenwood High, a feeder for all the
elementary schools in District 14. Hyde Park High was
going through a period of transition. Gangs were taking
over and enrollment had dropped. The Woodlawn
Organization, under the leadership of Leon Finney, was
organizing to turn the school around.

Dr. Ora McConner, the district's director of special
projects, Principal Beverly Weldon, and Leon Finney did
wonders at that school. It now enjoys a deservedly good
reputation.

Larry Hawkins, who directed the University of Chicago/
Hyde Park program, helped the youngsters develop
confidence and improve their scores on the college board
examinations.

My district was enlarged to include King High School,
4445 S. Drexel Blvd, and all of the elementary schools north
of Hyde Park. Now I had the poverty-area schools in the
Kenwood-Oakwood district, the middle-class schools in
Hyde Park and the schools in the activist community of
Woodlawn. I changed hats whenever I worked with
different groups. Each area had its own agenda.

Warren Bacon, a friend and former member of the
Chicago Board of Education, asked me to throw my name in
the hat to become a member of the Board of Education. I
had never thought about being on the board until then but I
realized I had an advantage over many of the other
candidates: I knew the language of the school system and
understood the major concerns of schools and community
alike.

Harold Washington, mayor of Chicago, gave the schoolboard tremendous support. He allowed us to move as far and as fast as we wanted to.

After Gardner's appointment to the school board was announced, he received a message from the former superintendent of schools, Joseph P. Hannon, dated April 26, 1984.

Dear Frank:

I read with much delight that Mayor Washington had appointed you to the school board. Every child in the system should be thrilled . . . because no better voice or friend will they ever have than you.

My best personal regards . . . if I may ever be of any assistance, please get in touch.

Joe

Frank's tenure on the board was not without fanfare and his performance paid off.

When it was learned that board president George Munoz was not available for another term, some of the board members asked me to become president. My colleagues on the board were in communication with the mayor, but Harold Washington did not talk to me about it at all. They kept him aware about what was going on at the board and arranged for the two of us to meet.

Mayor Washington asked me a few questions. He didn't know very much about me, but he knew my brother Edward and we had a pleasant interview.

Washington never once interfered with my administration during my tenure as president. This is quite different from the tone set by previous mayors. I was told by other board members and colleagues that his predecessor was constantly rapping board members over the knuckles, dictating their actions and orchestrating things they should do and not do and the things she wanted done. Mayor

Washington was quite a different person.

As president of the board, I spent a lot of time visiting schools. I would visit unannounced, making it a point of talking to the kids, both in high schools and elementary schools.

Looking back, I feel many things were accomplished during my tenure, but there was much more to be done. I learned a great deal on my odyssey from kindergarten to the presidency of the Chicago Public School system. My wish is that I have been a positive role model for many of the youngsters in our community.

Frank W. Gardner is very quiet, low-keyed and modest. Some of his critics have interpreted his style and demeanor as a weakness. They are wrong. Joy Darrow, former editor of the *Chicago Defender*, captured the essence of the man in her column of August 24, 1975: "The quiet ones are often the most effective."

A BLACK IN CORPORATE AMERICA WITHOUT A SPONSOR IS LIKE A SHIP WITHOUT A RUDDER

Walter H. Clark was born in Athens, Ga., June 5, 1928, the youngest son of John Quincy and Beulah Hill Clark. His parents were graduates of Wilberforce University, a traditional Black college in Wilberforce, Ohio. John Quincy, who earned a master's degree from the University of Illinois, taught, coached and subsequently became the principal of the Crispus Attucks High School for colored people in Carbondale, Ill., the school Walter and his brother John Quincy Jr. attended. The Clark brothers worked as *Chicago Defender* newspaper boys during their school years.

The white children in Carbondale attended Carbondale Community High School. Although the community of Carbondale only had two schools, it had two boards of education, one for the white school and another for the Black school. The Black school board was controlled by whites.

In 1946, during his senior year in high school, Walter was offered a football and basketball scholarship to Southern Illinois University in Carbondale. As the first Black to play on the SIU football team, he suffered many indignities. Walter could not accompany the team to play at Southeast Missouri State University in Cape Giradeau because the Missouri State team refused to play against a football team with a Black player.

Interstate basketball in Illinois was just as tainted with racism as interstate football. Black high school basketball teams were not permitted to participate in the annual Sweet Sixteen Basketball Tournament held in Champaign until 1953. Chicago's DuSable High School was the first Black team to break the color barrier.

The sting of racism that marred Walter's freshman year at Southern Illinois prompted him to transfer to the Compton Junior College in Compton, Calif., where he earned an associate of arts degree. He spent his third year at the University of California in Los Angeles. Walter could not afford to finish school on the West Coast, so he returned to SIU and received a bachelor's degree in business administration in 1951.

The white accounting students in Clark's senior class were able to secure work in small businesses in the surrounding towns, but there was no work in the Carbondale area for a Black accounting major.

Walter offered to work without pay for Mr. Curtis, a friend of his father's, in order to gain some on-the-job experience. Curtis, a member of the board of education, refused his request, saying that he was afraid that he would lose his client base if he had a Negro working on their books. John Clark Sr. reminded his friend Curtis that he was the only CPA in town and told him that it was unlikely that his clients would take the trouble to seek an accountant in another town. In spite of the Clarks' pleas, Curtis held to the position that having a Black on his staff would ruin his business.

The day after Walter graduated from SIU, he caught the first train going north to search for employment in Chicago. He went first to Howard Gould, a former Chicago Urban League industrial secretary, who operated an employment placement service at 412 E. 47th St. There were very few white-collar jobs above clerk/typist available to college-trained Blacks in the 1950s.

Gould gave Clark a number of leads at manufacturing companies and accounting firms. The CPA firms did not even extend him the courtesy of allowing him to fill out an application, while the manufacturing firms gave him a battery of tests, some of which took up to four hours to complete. The tests were really a charade for companies with government contracts that pretended to comply with the toothless Fair Employment Practices Commission (FEPC). For Walter, the results were always the same: he was over-educated for the positions that were available.

After months of searching for employment, Clark met Wilbur

Slaughter, a real estate broker who introduced him to Louise Quarles at the Illinois Federal Savings and Loan Association, a Black-owned institution located in the Rosenwald Building at 62 E. 47th St. Mrs. Quarles became Clark's immediate boss at Illinois Federal.

Robert R. Taylor, the secretary/treasurer of the association, was the first Black to be elected to the board of the Chicago Housing Authority. He served as its chairman from 1943 to 1950. Taylor's principal occupation was that of real estate manager of the Julius Rosenwald Michigan Boulevard Apartments, a post he held from 1927 to 1957.

Walter Clark had worked at Illinois Federal for six months when he was drafted into the U.S. Army. After eight weeks of basic training at Fort Riley, Kansas, he was sent to the adjutant general's school at Fort Benjamin Harrison, Ind., where he spent eight weeks learning typing and shorthand in preparation for work in administrative headquarters.

It was the custom at that time for graduates of the adjutant general's classes to select the posts where they would begin duty. The most popular locations were Rio de Janiero, Paris, Berlin, Madrid and London.

Walter Clark, the only Black among the 32 members of his group, did not have a choice. He alone received a direct order. The order was for him to be shipped immediately to Korea. Walter recalls:

> That was a helluva feeling. I felt like I was walking my last mile to the electric chair. White folks really know how to treat a Black. I was the only one in that group of 32 that had specific orders to go to a war zone. Although I had the highest test score in the group, I was the one who had to go to Korea.
>
> When I arrived in Korea, I told my superior I had just finished the adjutant general's school. The sergeant said, 'I don't give a damn what you finished.' He handed me a rifle and said, 'This is land duty over here. We don't need any adjutant generals. This ain't no place to take shorthand.'
>
> I told him I was really at a disadvantage because most of the soldiers who were in Korea had been trained for at least 16 weeks as a combat unit.
>
> Since I had no success at getting my message through to the company officers, I wrote letters to Congressman

William L. Dawson, D-Ill., and U.S. Sen. Paul H. Douglas,
D-Ill. I explained to them that my life was imperiled
because I had not had proper training for the infantry and
told them how much money the government had spent to
teach me office skills rather than combat tactics.

By the time I was finally transferred to an
administrative position in a quartermaster's division, the
shooting war was over. The only advantage that came out of
the transfer was that it gave me several opportunities to
visit Japan.

In 1954, after I was discharged, I went back to work at
Illinois Federal, where I had previously kept books and also
acted as a teller in the morning. I solicited new accounts in
the evening, and on weekends I spoke at organizations and
churches to acquaint people with the services that were
being offered by the association.

I learned that my position as bookkeeper at Illinois
Federal had been taken over by a young lady and they
wanted to cut my salary. Using the directives from the
Army, I explained that they couldn't cut my salary nor could
they refuse to rehire me because I had been drafted and had
not volunteered for Army duty.

It was clear from the day I returned to work that
someone at Illinois Federal didn't like me. I started looking
around for another job.

I also registered at DePaul University, Chicago, and
started working on my master's degree. It was at the DePaul
personnel placement center that I heard about an opening at
First Federal Savings and Loan Association of Chicago. A
lady in the placement center told me that she knew they had
openings, but she also knew that they didn't have any Blacks
working there. I told her I would like to try anyway.

I filed my application with First Federal and was
interviewed by Morton Bodfish, the chairman. I thought it
was kind of unique for the chairman of a major institution
to interview an applicant for a clerical job.

I made it a point to tell Mr. Bodfish that I was still
working at Illinois Federal and asked him to keep the
interview confidential.

However, the very next morning, Mr. Taylor greeted me

at the door of Illinois Federal and said, 'I hear you were down at First Federal.'

'Who, me?'

'Yes. Morton Bodfish called to see what kind of fellow you are,' he replied. 'I'm sure if you go back down there, you will have a job.'

I followed Mr. Taylor's advice and became the first Black to be hired by First Federal.

The time was May 1955. I was lonesome. I had no contacts there except the chairman.

My first position at First Federal was that of an accounting clerk. The most difficult thing about it was that I had no sponsors, no one to show me the ropes or provide a support system. It was like being thrown into water loaded with barracudas. My options were to swim faster than hell or be eaten alive. I swam.

Another discouraging thing about the job was the fact that although I had a pretty good education and majored in accounting, my immediate boss had not even finished high school. I swallowed hard and made the adjustment because there really were no other white-collar jobs available in an industry that blatantly practiced racism in lending.

Racism frequently comes under the guise of friendship. The director of personnel at First Federal was a vice president who appeared to be worried about my marital status. A week did not pass without her asking me when I was going to get married. She was overly concerned about how well my courtship was going, but I thought she had a genuine interest in me. I didn't have any reason to think anything else.

I had been on the job about four or five months when the company had a dance. One of the girls who worked in the personnel division danced with me.

The personnel vice president called me into her office the first thing the next morning and asked: 'Why were you dancing with that girl?'

'Well, what's the problem?' I asked her.

She said, 'I just think it's wrong for you to ask a young lady for a dance without really giving her a chance to make a selection. She probably didn't want to dance with you, but since you asked her, she didn't want to hurt your feelings. I don't really feel that it's right for you to put that kind of pressure on a young lady.'

Clark let the woman talk until she exhausted the subject. Then he said:

'It just so happens that the young lady asked me to dance. I didn't ask her.' The woman didn't know what to say. She simply looked flabbergasted. It was then that I realized her concern about my getting married was really a fear of my socializing with white women.

Several months after I was hired at First Federal, I decided to drop all of my moonlighting accounting jobs and concentrate on building a good reputation with that institution. I earned a MBA, but in spite of my best efforts, I didn't really begin to move up the corporate ladder until after I had been aboard about eight years.

In 1963, I was promoted in the accounting department, not as its head but as a supervisor. I worked for the acting treasurer. The man had not graduated from college. My duties included preparing data information for my boss to present to the board of directors. Before every board meeting he would ask me for an analysis of certain transactions, which I always supplied.

Frequently he was unable to understand the information I presented to him.

One day one of the board members asked my boss who prepared the material. He said, 'Walter did.' A board member asked, 'Who the hell is Walter?' and added that the board wanted to see the person who was turning out the reports. 'Go get Walter,' he instructed. So I went to the board meeting and explained the report.

My supervisor was not happy in his role of acting treasurer. He really was not qualified and he didn't want the job. However, the guy that he reported to told him if he didn't stay on, they would offer the position to me. So he kept the job because he didn't want to report to a Black man.

I became treasurer of the association in 1967 when the

acting treasurer shifted into a data processing job that he liked.

Back in those years, First Federal/American Legion Post held an annual party when new officers were installed. The year I was promoted, they had picked out one of the popular new restaurants on the near North Side. I had to make all the arrangements for the party by phone, including the menu.

Shortly after arriving at the restaurant, I told the maitre'd that I would be responsible for the check. He stared at me and said, 'We don't allow Negroes in here.' I said, 'Well, I'm the treasurer of the organization. I don't see how we're going to have dinner and install the officers unless you allow me to stay.'

He said, 'I'm sorry, that's the rule.'

So I told the guys that we had to leave. We all filed out and went back to the office and had the installation.

In 1968, Morton Bodfish, the chairman of the savings and loan association, was taken ill. The directors decided to search outside of the First Federal structure for his replacement.

The new chairman was Stanley Enlund, who came over from the Sears Bank and Trust Co. The guys I reported to were angry because they didn't get the chairmanship. They would not speak to Mr. Enlund, they wouldn't help him, they wouldn't give him any directions. I said to my wife Juanita, 'This doesn't make sense. This fellow Enlund is the chairman. He is going to be the one that will make the final evaluations on the top guys and decide who and how much each individual will be paid.' My better judgement told me to speak to him.

The next day, I went into his office, introduced myself and described my duties at the bank. He appreciated my gesture and acknowledged it in many ways as the years passed.

Stan Enlund geared the company to move along quite smoothly, in part because he approved some innovations that I made. He set a precedent by skipping over the First Federal officers and selecting a new president who was really not a banker but an educator. Grover Hansen had a

MBA from the University of Chicago.

As I look back at that period, the whole savings and loan industry had been filled with people who had very little formal education. Hansen started opening things up by seeking out educated people with new ideas.

With Stan as chairman and Grover as the new president, I began to get some breaks that I earned by working my butt off to understand that business. I knew the regulations, and when they came to me for all kinds of information and sought my advice, I knew they appreciated my judgment and capabilities. I finally felt comfortable in my niche at First Federal.

I wasn't the type of person who would go around advertising my accomplishments, and that possibly was one of my mistakes. However, you can promote yourself in various ways. I'm not talking about holding up a sign and walking around saying I'm great. I'm talking about demonstrating to your superiors that you know what you are doing. That's selling yourself to whomever you work for, to the board members or anyone else.

I began to do that. Many times I shared some good ideas with my superiors and they presented them to the board. That really made me feel good, and they, in turn, felt good about me. I didn't say these were Walter Clark's ideas. Joe Blow was my conduit and I let him present it to the board. It was during that period that I really began to feel that I had a sponsor at First Federal and that I had earned that sponsor because I was producing. I was made vice president and treasurer of the institution in late 1969.

The officers of First Federal had the use of memberships in a number of private clubs, where they entertained clients. The coordinator of these activities was Jim Fitzmorris, who had a membership at the Mid-America Club. On one occasion, I called Fitzmorris and said that I had a broker coming in from New York and I'd like to use the membership.

Jim said, 'Okay, I'll see if I can connect that up.' But instead of calling Mid-America, he called Stan Enlund. 'I don't think they allow Black people there,' he told him. 'Walter wants to take one of his clients over there for lunch. What should I do?'

Stan called me to his office and said, 'I hear you want to take so and so over to the Mid-America Club.' I told him, 'Yes. This fellow from New York has been nice to me and I think he would enjoy dining at the club.'

'Can't you find some other place to take him,' Stan asked.

'I'm sure I could,' I replied. 'But I want to take him where it's not too loud, where there's a nice atmosphere and excellent food.'

He said, 'Well, Walter, they don't allow Blacks to invite people over there.'

'I've been over there to affairs that we have given,' I retorted.

He said, 'Yes, you can be a guest but you cannot invite a guest.'

I said, 'That doesn't quite make sense, Stan.'

He said, 'It may not make sense, but that's their rule.'

'If that's their rule, I don't think we should have a membership there,' I told him. 'If all of our officers cannot participate—because it's not just Jim Fitzmorris' membership, it's really First Federal's membership—I don't think any of us should have a membership.'

'Well, don't get too hasty,' he cautioned. 'Just settle down.'

I said, 'I'm not that hyped up on going but I think it's wrong. I am at a disadvantage as an officer if I can't entertain clients there like the rest of you.'

This author recalls during the late 1960s and early '70s, Arthur Rubloff, the real estate tycoon, invited me to a number of affairs he held at the Mid-America Club. And for the longest time whenever I'd go, the white parking attendants thought I was a chauffeur even though I have never worn a cap or uniform of any kind except in the Army.

The parkers would invariably rush up to my car and ask, 'Who are you here to pick up?' To avoid giving an explanation that they possibly would not have understood, I would say, 'The boss and he's upstairs.'

That was language that was very clear to them. They just couldn't conceptualize—even after I verbally blessed them out for their stupidity on several occasions—that a Black would have any reason to pull into the reserved section of the garage except as somebody's driver. To them, any Black who showed up had to be driving somebody, even if it was not Miss Daisy, because Miss Daisy couldn't be a member of that club either.

Walter continues:

Stan must have given some thought about the club membership after our conversation because in 1970 he sponsored Fred Ford of Draper and Kramer as a member in the Union League Club. Twelve months later he sponsored me.

That organization required applicants to have three main sponsors and other references and to go through an interview process.

Stan was so nervous about the possibility that I may be turned down that he looked for me every morning and asked, 'Well, how are things going? Have they set up your interview date yet? I sure hope you make it.'

I would reassure him: 'Stan, relax. The world did not begin and will not end with the Union League Club.'

I was accepted and became the second Black to hold membership in the Union League. I really take my hat off to Stan for taking the necessary steps to get us in. Membership in a prestigious club makes a difference in the corporate world.

However, even as a member, some funny things happen to me. Even now, when I go over there with a white guest, some waiters automatically give the guest the bill.

It was at the Union League Club over lunch that I came up with the idea that we set up a treasury division at First Federal to deal with Treasury bonds, notes and bills. Although I didn't report directly to the chairman, I made my proposal available to him, along with suggestions on how to operate the new treasury division.

When I discussed my proposal with Mr. Enlund I put in my bid to head the new department, adding that I would only need a secretary and one other person to get it in operation. I told him that once it got rolling, which I anticipated would take two years, I wanted to return to my position as supervisor of the accounting department. I didn't want to be in a specialized operation, I wanted line responsibility. The chairman approved my revolutionary idea of a savings and loan entering the bond market.

I had learned everything I knew about operating a treasury division through study and discussions over the phone. I got a real education just over the telephone. Of course, the idea was new to people in the capital market and they were eager to explore the potentials with me. To my knowledge, we were the first ones in the savings and loan industry to ever invest in federal funds.

I began trading through the Chase Manhattan Bank of New York. Thomas G. LaBrecque, who helped me set up our account, is now the president of Chase. He was excited about the opportunity and said he would be buying and selling fed funds every day. I sent him $5 million to open an account and had a transaction ready to go the first day that the regulations became viable. I had done my homework.

Clark's big move came in 1973 when he was appointed a member of the board of directors and was promoted to senior vice president and financial group manager. As the chief financial officer, he was responsible for managing approximately $1.3 billion in assets. He had six senior officers reporting to him in the areas of mortgage lending, the investment portfolio, data processing, income tax policy and returns, financial planning and analysis, general accounting, budgeting and loan accounting.

In 1977, when he was made executive vice president, Clark became one of the top three officers at First Federal Savings and Loan Association of Chicago. Clark states:

> As the third man in line, many of Stan's and Grover's important telephone calls were shifted to me in their absence. One afternoon, Arthur Rubloff called for Stan. When the secretary told him Mr. Enlund was not in the office, Mr. Rubloff said, 'Let me talk to Grover.' 'He's not here either,' she replied.
>
> 'Who can I talk to?' Rubloff asked. 'I will give you to Mr. Clark. He's next in line,' responded the secretary. 'Okay, let me talk to Clark.'
>
> He said, 'Clark, I couldn't get Enlund and Hansen. I

have a situation here we need some help on.' 'What's the trouble, Arthur?' I asked.

'You know the Evergreen Park Plaza shopping center I built out south on 95th and Western Avenue?'

'Yes.'

'My heart and soul is in there,' he said. 'We got a church out there that whites are moving out of and some Blacks want to purchase it. We just can't have that.'

'We can't have what?'

'We can't have the Blacks purchasing that church,' Rubloff retorted. 'We've got to do something. I'm trying to get a group together to put down some money so we can stop the Blacks from moving in. I don't want anything in that community that is going to affect my shopping center. You just have to face it, whites don't like Blacks and Blacks don't like whites. I ain't going to try and change all of that. I ain't got enough time to live to do all of that. We need a couple hundred thousand from you. I'm gonna put in some and I've got some other people putting up money so we can buy this church. We'll decide later what we're going to do with it. But we cannot let those Blacks purchase that property.'

'I will deliver your message,' I told him.

After a brief pause, Rubloff asked, 'What's your name again?' I said, 'Walter Clark.'

The author and Walter Clark knew the late Arthur Rubloff as a man who loved Chicago and all its people, a tycoon who contributed millions of dollars to hospitals, museums and other Chicago institutions. Arthur's heart was bigger than the derby he usually wore.

Rubloff said he would not live long enough to solve the race problem—and he didn't. But it is my belief that the solution to the race problem is in the hands of men like Rubloff, the captains of America's industry.

Walter Clark's rise in the corporate ranks demonstrates that the philosophy of fairness, wherever it is practiced, can make a difference if it mandated from the top level. Clark would be the first one to testify that he has had to mud wrestle with some white folks, but he will also admit that fair-minded whites were responsible for the opportunities in which he could forge an outstanding career in a tough industry.

IN A BLACK MAN'S HAND, TWO DOCTORATES MAY NOT BE ENOUGH

Robert C. Stepto was born in Chicago October 6, 1920, in Provident Hospital, located at 29th Street and Dearborn Avenue, 15 months after the Chicago race riot in the bloody summer of 1919. He was the eldest of the four children of Robert Louis and Grace Elvie (Williams) Stepto. The earliest address Robert remembers is 4949 S. Forrestville Ave. The Steptos lived at that address when his father, a postal employee, injured his hand. Little Robert accompanied his dad when he rushed to the office of their family physician, Dr. Pedro M. Santos. The boy observed the doctor treating his father's hand, amazed with the wizardry of medicine. He was fascinated: the healing was almost like magic.

That incident even affected Robert's playtime. While the other children argued over who would be cowboys and who would be Indians, Bob always played the doctor who attended to the wounded on the battlefield.

Young Stepto was destined to be the first physician in either parent's family. He never considered any other profession during the difficult times ahead.

Robert attended Wendell Phillips Elementary School at 38th and Prairie until the family moved to 6350 S. Vernon, in Woodlawn. He refers to Woodlawn as the "silk stocking district" because many of its residents were professionals, school teachers and civil service workers. His new school was McCosh Elementary, where he graduated with honors in June 1934.

Bob attended Englewood High School, where white students were the majority, and graduated among the top 10 of the June 1938 class at the age of 17. He accepted a scholarship at Northwestern University.

Bob had no real concept of racism and isolation until he began classes on the Evanston campus of the university:

> There were only 15 Black students on campus that semester. I still remember Clarence Hinton; Bernard Jefferson, the outstanding running back in 1937-38; and Helen V. Payne, who also became a physician.
>
> During my first year at the university, I commuted on the elevated train between the Evanston campus and my home on the South Side of Chicago. During my second year I got lucky and found a job as an orderly at the Evanston Community Hospital.
>
> Community, founded by Dr. Isabelle Garnett and two other physicians, was the only hospital in the area that would admit Black patients. My wages were $3.50 a week, but Dr. Garnett also arranged for me to have a sleeping room rent free. It wasn't a bad proposition because there were no housing facilities on the Northwestern University campus for Blacks.
>
> All I did was work and study, principally study. I was so satisfied with the arrangement that I decided to go to school year-round in order to protect my job and sleeping quarters.
>
> I maintained a high grade point average in spite of the fact that I worked six hours every night, six nights a week. Even with my work and class load, I never gave a thought to not being able to meet my objective of going to medical school.
>
> It was not until my junior year when my advisor, Mr. Bochstahler, asked, 'Why are you in pre-med?'
>
> I said, 'Because I want to be a doctor.'
>
> He said that as bright as I was I should have known that they would not accept Blacks at the Northwestern University Medical School. 'You can't apply here at

Northwestern,' he said. 'You can't apply at the University of Illinois. So where are you going to go to school?' I told him I was going to apply wherever I could as long as I could manage to scrape up the application fees.

Mr. Bochstahler acknowledged that I had pretty good grades, but warned that my dream of going to medical school could turn into a nightmare.

As far as I was concerned, Bochstahler could have saved his breath. I knew I was going to go to medical school and become a physician.

I applied to Howard University in Washington, D.C., the University of Wisconsin in Madison, and the University of Illinois, Champaign/Urbana. I wasn't too bent on going to the University of Illinois because I suffered with asthma. I frequently had asthma attacks in Chicago but was never bothered by them in Evanston. So I decided the best thing for me was to get out of the state if I could afford it.

I had never given serious thought to being able to afford to move. Then Lady Luck and her companion hard work tapped me on the shoulders once again and I was offered a scholarship at the Howard Medical School beginning in the fall of 1941, providing I maintained my grade point average at Northwestern until graduation.

I was second on the waiting list at the University of Wisconsin but decided Howard would be my best bet because of the scholarship. Another factor was that my fiance Ann Burns had relatives in Washington with whom I could live without any additional expense.

Lady Luck was with me once more: I took advantage of the U.S. Army Specialized Training Program (ASTP), which assumed the tuition for men eligible to serve in the armed forces who had IQ scores of 115 or better. The program allowed me to graduate from medical school without going directly into the military service.

Ann and I were married during my junior year at medical school and that made a great difference in where I would have my internship. My parents wanted me to come back to Chicago, although I had accepted an internship at Jersey City Medical in New Jersey. I had also been offered internships at Homer G. Phillips Hospital in St. Louis and at Provident Hospital in Chicago. I decided to come back to Chicago. Ann didn't want to leave her beautiful city by the lake, and she was the real persuader.

It appears that good things were falling in my path. Soon after I returned to Chicago, Franklin McLean at the University of Chicago developed a plan called the Provident Medical Fellowship that subsequently became the National Medical Fellowship. It was a project organized to improve opportunities for Blacks who wanted to enter special medical training. I completed my internship at Provident in 1945, and did my residency in obstetrics and gynecology in a combined program with Provident and the University of Chicago Lying-In Hospital.

After completing my residency requirements, I arranged for an interview with Dr. William Dieckman, who was the chairman of the OB-GYN department at the University of Chicago. I had not been forewarned of his prejudice, but I got an inkling that something was wrong after he kept me waiting in the reception area for two hours.

The first words out of his mouth when I entered his office were, 'Well, I see you have an application in and you want to come here.' That was obvious, I thought to myself. 'What particular phase of obstetrics are you interested in working in?' he asked.

I said, 'Toxaemia pregnancy.'

'We do not know a lot about the pathology of toxaemia pregnancy,' he said.

I retorted, 'My interest is in the whole pathology involved in obstetrics and gynecology.'

'I don't know if we can do anything for you here,' he said. 'However, if you can get accepted by the graduate school at the University of Chicago, I'll accept you.'

'You mean I have to go back to graduate school after having completed seven years above the undergraduate level?' I gasped.

'That's right.'

I had a friend who taught in the U of C pathology department. Dr. Robert Stewart Jason was the second Black person to get a Ph.D. in pathology at the University of Chicago. The first one was Julian Lewis, M.D., Ph.D., who recently died at the ripe old age of 96.

Dr. Jason wrote a letter to the chairman of the department confirming that all my credentials were in order and I enrolled in the master's program in pathology at the university.

I completed my course work for the master's in nine months and I went back to Dr. Dieckman because I wanted to get some clinical experience in the hospital. After I acquainted him with the fact that I was qualified for a master's in pathology, he said, 'That's nice, but you need additional education. All of the other residents here are doing research projects because that's the thrust of an academic institution. If you want to see patients, you need to go to the Stockyard Clinic, which is over behind the back of the yards area near 47th and Ashland.'

Dr. Dieckman had recommended the Stockyard Clinic because they handled a large number of Black patients. I will have to chalk it up to naivete that it had not dawned on me that the white establishment did not want Black doctors treating white women.

I didn't appreciate his telling me I needed more courses when my laboratory work in pathology was more additional training than 50 percent of the white residents had taken. In addition, it was blatantly racist to steer me to a "for colored only" medical situation. My hands were tied and I was at the end of the gang plank, so I spent another year in academia.

My fellowship in the department of pathology was renewed, so with my head held high, I completed the requirements for my master's and Ph.D. in 24 months.

The problem I had while studying at the University of Chicago was that many physicians there wouldn't speak to me. When I gave them a friendly hello they would act as if I were the invisible man. I'd go to conferences and they'd look through me or glare like I was a creature from another planet. It seems that the only white persons I had contact with were the cadavers I encountered in Pathology 501.

It was during those extended periods in the pathology lab that I discovered I was alone but I was not lonely. To me being lonely means that you are susceptible to depression and the negatives that go with it. But you can be alone in a group and be into yourself. Being lonely you have no interactions, no self-esteem. Being alone, you can accomplish a lot as long as you have the inner strength to deal with racism. A good example is a man in the wilderness. He is alone but he is not necessarily lonely.

After I received my Ph.D. in pathology in 1948, the University of Chicago Hospital still would not accept me in any capacity. There was no room in their inn for me. Two doctorates were not enough for a Black man to enter those doors. I was out in the wilderness without a job.

Dr. Rachmiel Levine, a physician who was called the father of modern medical research in endocrinology, invited me to join him in the lab at Michael Reese Hospital. 'Bob, he said, 'Come work with me because I hear you're catching hell.'

My experiences during two years at Michael Reese were productive. During that time, I shared an office suite with an internist, Nathaniel Calloway, M.D. and Ph.D., at 5751 S. Indiana Ave. Also practicing out of that office were Dr. William Cunningham, an internal medicine man and Dr. Mack Tanner, a dentist who had offices on the second floor.

I was so busy in the clouds of academia that I didn't fully realize the responsibilities of a man with a wife and a young child. One afternoon, my wife said that we could use some additional money and reminded me that people often asked if I would make house calls. I told her I couldn't make house calls because I didn't have a bag. She got me a bag. So I started seeing patients in their homes in the evening.

I worked out an arrangement at Michael Reese Hospital under which I could enter private practice without jeopardizing my fellowship from the U.S. Public Health Service. After I completed two years of research at Reese, I applied for a staff appointment, which was refused. The only Black doctor I know who had a staff appointment at Reese until that time was Henry I. Wilson. After his death around 1952, a decade passed before a Black physician received an appointment at Reese.

After I had been rejected for a staff appointment at Michael Reese Hospital, Dr. Michael Levine told me that I could stay on and work with him in the lab and make a living. I said, 'I can't make a living in the research lab. And I'm qualified to earn much more than what Reese is paying me.'

Dr. Harry Boysen, head of the OB-GYN department at Presbyterian-St. Luke's asked me to come on board as the director of his training program, but said that he did not want me to bring in any Black patients. They would pay me something like $12,000 or $14,000 a year, but I said that was only four times the amount of money I received on a fellowship and spurned that offer. Provident Hospital offered me an appointment as head of the OB-GYN, which I accepted.

Dr. Herbert Schmitz at Lewis Memorial Hospital, 30th Street and Michigan Avenue, offered me a faculty appointment at Loyola University and hospital privileges at Lewis Memorial. I accepted with the provisions that I could work with him in the cytology laboratory, where I could continue my basic research and also see my patients. I worked with Schmitz until about 1960. Samuel Cardinal Strich decided to close the hospital when Dr. Schmitz died.

After the demise of Lewis Memorial, I joined the Mercy Hospital staff and encountered real pressure. The medical people did not want a Black on the staff at that hospital. I had been dropped from the Loyola faculty shortly after Schmitz died and needed a new faculty appointment in order to keep the staff position at Mercy. The University of Illinois filled the bill: they made me an associate professor.

In 1953, Nathaniel Calloway and I became founding members of the Medical Associates, along with Drs. Robert L. Kimbrough, William Rogers and Mack Tanner, all practicing dentists. Dr. Clay Jones came in with Dr. Ollie Crawford in pediatrics. Dr. John Coleman and Dr. Robert Morris were the radiologists. Dr. Aubry Manley joined Calloway and Cunningham in internal medicine. Dr. James Richardson was the opthalmalogist.

The Medical Associates was the first Black group of its kind to be organized for the practice of medicine in Chicago. We had a suite of offices in the new Lake Meadows complex at 3233 S. King Dr. The corporation had a general manager and its own pharmacist and laboratory technicians. Dr.

Calloway was the group leader and entrepreneur. He became president of the Chicago Urban League in 1955.

I applied again for a staff appointment at Michael Reese because it was in back of the Medical Associates' office facility. They rejected me again. They haven't accepted me until this day, though I must admit I have not applied lately.

By 1962, racism had mounted two frontal attacks in the medical profession: suppression of Black physicians and exploitation of Black patients. Relief was sought in the courts. Suits were filed against many of the hospitals that would not accept Black patients and Black doctors. White doctors had begun to siphon off Black patients to hospitals where Black doctors were not allowed to practice, despite their qualifications.

Racism in medicine is no different from the racial prejudice in other facets of Black life in America. It is a virus that visits the Black population in differing degrees of intensity every two, four, six and eight decades. It is a deliberate effort by the white establishment to keep the Black population busy reinventing the wheel. How else can you explain why Robert C. Stepto was told by his student advisor in 1940 that Blacks were not acceptable at the Northwestern Medical School at the very time that Theodore K. Lawless, an internationally renowned dermatologist, served on its faculty from 1924 to 1941? Dr. Lawless was one of several Blacks who had received medical degrees from Northwestern in the early 1900s.

Dr. Lawless was denied in-patient privileges at Northwestern's Wesley Memorial Hospital, Chicago, but his world-wide reputation drew white patients from many countries to seek treatment at his three-story white brick office building at 4321 S. Parkway. It has been estimated that 80 percent of his patients were white. The author has witnessed patients of every hue waiting in lines that stretched halfway around the block to consult the doctor who had become a legend in his own time. Dr. Lawless, who treated rich and poor, white and Black, without discrimination charged them all a standard fee of $5.00. The physician did not believe in segregating money or people.

Dr. Stepto shares his views on segregation:

The housing of Black patients in hospitals mirrored the Jim Crow patterns of our society at large. For example, at the

Illinois Central Hospital, which is now Hyde Park
Community Hospital, Black patients were kept in the
basement by agreement with the Illinois Central Railroad.
The Negro patients' beds were approximately four rooms
removed from where we performed autopsies on cadavers.
This was a terrible situation.

There were segregated wards at the General Hospital in
Washington, D.C. I recall when we made rounds at St.
Elizabeth Hospital, a mental institution in the District of
Columbia, they had floors for Blacks and floors for whites.

Lying-In Hospital at the University of Chicago had the
Max Epstein area, which housed Black patients on the south
side of the building. The upper floors of the hospital were
reserved for white patients.

Segregation was minimal at Cook County Hospital
because of its heavy patient loads. Lewis Memorial, like
many other hospitals, dodged the segregation problem by
placing Black patients in private rooms. At the South
Chicago Hospital, the Black patient was an anomaly for so
long that they were simply accepted. Black and white wards
existed for a long time. It was not until about 1969 or '70
that we began to see the open-bed policy practiced in a
hospital.

Today you can walk through hospitals and find little
discrimination in the assignment of beds. This is due to two
pressures: economic pressure from Blacks who can afford to
pay for top medical service, and pressure from courts and
activists to end discrimination in health care. However,
there are still some white doctors who refuse to permit their
patients to share a room with a Black. Their motto is
segregation yesterday, segregation today, segregation
tomorrow, segregation forever.

I made some effort to alleviate segregation by
appointing a white doctor from Woodlawn Hospital to the
Provident Hospital staff.

It's strange that I got on the staff at the Woodlawn
Hospital by the back door. One of my patients was carried
to the emergency room at the Woodlawn Hospital because
she was bleeding profusely. The doctors there said that I
was on the staff, though I never had been. They called me

and asked that I come over immediately to see this patient. While I was there they asked me whether I'd join them. That is how I became the first Black doctor on the staff of Woodlawn Hospital.

A year later, John Harrod, who had been a resident in OB-GYN at the University of Chicago when I was studying pathology there, asked me to join the staff at South Chicago Hospital. The hospital was attempting to qualify for an accredited OB-GYN program. Since I had been board certified in OB-GYN since 1952 and John Harrod was also certified, we were directly responsible for South Chicago Hospital getting accreditation. I didn't have time to do a lot of work out there. I did some surgery and a few deliveries. At least some of my white peers had opportunities to see a Black physician perform under all kinds of circumstances.

In 1968, I became chairman of the department of obstetrics and gynecology at the Chicago Medical School. When Chicago Medical School and Mt. Sinai merged, I was asked to become chairman at Mt. Sinai. The first day that I came on board, several white physicians decided they wanted to take their patients some place else. They moved their practices to Skokie, Highland Park and other North Shore locations. The majority of the staff supported me and I ran both programs.

Chicago Medical School has a significant place in medical history for Black folks in particular and Americans in general. Dr. Stepto was appointed chairman of the OB-GYN department exactly 85 years after Dr. Daniel Hale Williams graduated from that institution. Dr. Williams, one of America's greatest surgeons, pioneered open heart surgery. In 1893, he performed open heart surgery on James Cornish at Provident Hospital, where Dr. Stepto was born almost three decades later. Dr. Williams further distinguished himself by creating the first Negro nursing school at Freedman's Hospital in Washington, D.C., before the turn of the century. He alone was responsible for the policy adopted by Provident Hospital in 1891, which opened the hospital to all qualified physicians without regard to color. In 1898 and '99, Dr. Williams was the first Negro to hold a post at St. Luke's Hospital and Northwestern Hospital.

Dr. Stepto, like Dr. Lawless and Dr. Williams, has made significant contributions in his field of medicine. Stepto's talents were in great demand:

> I was approached by the Health and Governing Commission at the Cook County Hospital to become its chairman, and told that I could maintain my chairmanships at Mt. Sinai and the Chicago Medical School. I thought about about all the work involved in operating from three posts, but I took the position because I considered it a challenge. I found out one thing while holding three chairmanships at once: the more power you have, the more respect you get regardless of the color of your skin.
>
> I took advantage of my position to appoint women, Black and white, to programs where they had never been appointed before. We also managed to get more Blacks in the residency programs, both at County and Mt. Sinai.
>
> I think these were important steps toward opening many of the opportunities that we have today, although there still are not as many as there should be.
>
> Mt. Sinai separated from the Chicago Medical School, which moved to Downey, Ill. Chicago Medical wanted me to follow them to their new location and recruit students and residents for their program, but that was impossible. I resigned from the school and kept my chairmanships at Mt. Sinai and at Cook County.
>
> Merger mania was in the air: the teaching faculty of Rush-Presbyterian-St. Luke's and Mt. Sinai merged. I was a full professor at Rush-Pres until 1979 and resigned from Mt. Sinai in order to accept the position as the director of gynecology and gynecological surgery at the University of Chicago.
>
> To me, that move held several implications. Financially it was a step down, but morally I felt this was something I had to do because it brought me full circle to a hospital that had refused to let me perform any clinical work as recently as 30 years ago. From a professional point of view, it was a positive move because it signified to colleagues in my specialty all over the country that there are competent Blacks operating at the very senior level in the field of medicine.

It also was an opportunity to serve as a role model for young Black students and doctors, and to show that one can achieve in spite of man-made barriers.

Whenever democracy is attained in our nation—on any level—it benefits all Americans.

TODAY'S RACISM IS A BEACON FOR THE 21ST CENTURY

The noose of racism will continue to hold the American mind in bondage deep into the 21st century unless America makes a deep U-Turn in its race relations. The racial mindset that prevails over white America presently in the academic arena and other public and private institutions is casting a large and dark shadow over generations to come.

Black children born in the post-civil rights era are experiencing racial tensions similar to those that plagued their parents and grandparents. The intensity of overt racial hatred has escalated in the Reagan-Bush era. George Bush's "thousand points of light" were not the sunburst of hope some of us had envisioned; instead, they reflect burning crosses ignited by the fear and prejudice harbored by Klansmen in pin-striped suits and their latter-day counterparts, the Skinheads.

When Ronald Reagan took office in 1981, conservative and extreme right-wing voices grew stronger and louder on college and university campuses across the face of America. The most strident of the voices came from the pages of the *Dartmouth Review*. Although the *Review* is independent of Dartmouth College, Hanover, N.H., it is the product of Dartmouth students.

Chris Baldwin, who in 1982 was a junior at the college and the editor of the *Dartmouth Review*, argued that: Dartmouth College should be a meritocracy. "Whether you are a child of an alumni member, whether you happen to be Black or Hispanic or a woman, that's irrelevant," he said. "What counts is merit. What have you done? Who are you? Why should Dartmouth let you in?"

In 1982, the *Review* published a satire of Black students at Dartmouth that sent shockwaves through the college:

Dese boys be sayin' that we be comin' here to Darmut an not takin' the classics. You know, Homa, Shakesphere; but I hea' day all be co'd in da ground, six fee unda' and whatcha be askin' us to learn from dem? We be culturally 'lightened too. We be takin' hard courses in many subjects, like Afro-Am Studies, Women's studies and Policy studies. And who be mouthin' 'bout us not bein' good read? I be practily knowin' *Roots* cova to cova, til' my mine be boogying to da words! An' I be watchin' the Jeffersons on tv till I be blue in da face.

Gregory Ricks, former assistant dean at Dartmouth, said:

When I read the article the first time, with 'we be dis and we be dat, to me this that and the other,' it was like a bad joke. It was something that came from old films like, *Birth of the Nation*, or something like that. Nobody could even deal with this in any serious kind of way in these times, especially at a place like Dartmouth College. To me, it was almost out of the Dark Ages.

Chris Baldwin championed the article:

The bottom line is that there are some students here at Dartmouth who do not speak proper English, and that is sad. It's because they haven't been afforded the same opportunities as other students. But we cannot admit people at Dartmouth who are lower and less academically qualified than other students. And the heat and explosive attention that the article generated is because that satire was so effective. It went right for the jugular.

The *Review* is an equal opportunity attacker, making no discrimination between minority students and minority faculty members. William Cole, who teaches a Black studies course called "Music II," is a regular target. A 1983 *Review* editorial attacked Mr. Cole for his repeated references to race and described him as "a used Brillo pad."

In 1987, the *Review* named Mr. Cole as one of the worst professors at Dartmouth, describing his teaching methods as "a cross between that of a welfare queen and a bathroom attendant." The *Review's* barrages have gained no support from the Dartmouth administration and faculty, who value Mr. Cole as a more-than-competent colleague.

Professor Cole has been walking on a thin line from the first day he stepped into a classroom at Dartmouth, but his burden is much lighter than that of some Black students who are victimized by both the faculty and their peers.

Lary Lewman, the narrator for the Frontline WGBH production of "Racism: 101," which was broadcast on public television May 10, 1988, reported: "The influence of the *Review* has reached far beyond this small New Hampshire town. It has won large contributions from alumni, and its success has spawned imitators on campuses across the country. Its graduates have gone on to influential jobs: one became a speech writer for President Reagan, another for Vice President Bush. The man who signed the original jive column is now a speech writer for the Secretary of Education. The man who published the column became a policy analyst for the Reagan White House."

The Reagan appointments to the Supreme Court and to the White House signified that the time is ripe to spew the venom of bigotry from towers constructed to be lighthouses of enlightenment. The young and thoughtless in search of a leader have taken their cues from the ensconced administration. Campuses are writhing with unrest; some have been the scenes of mock lynchings. Although physical lynchings by mobs outside of the police force in America have dropped from few to none in the past decades, verbal lynchings of Black students are becoming commonplace.

Carl T. Rowan, the nationally syndicated columnist of the *Chicago Sun-Times*, responded to the racism that is taking place on college campuses:

> I cannot ask the media to stop reporting on the Skinheads and Kluxes and their outrages on 'white' campuses. What's news is news. And that is part of the educating of America.

I can ask brilliant young Blacks to be brave and not turn
campuses over to bigots by default. I can ask the best and
brightest of Blacks to say, 'Oberlin, Yale, the University of
Massachusetts are part of my birth right. I will not allow a
few bigots to reimpose Jim Crow in any area simply because
I capitulated to intimidation.'

A recent example occurred at Loyola University, a Jesuit institution in Chicago. Sophomore Sandra R. Westmoreland was enrolled in
Philosophy-Business Ethics 203. On January 22, 1990, Dr. Alfred Gini,
the instructor, discussed eight factors that make it difficult for some
people to comprehend and adopt ethical behavior. One of the reasons,
he said, was bad habits. The professor cited an example:

There was an old Southern white man who had held a
teaching position in a university. The old man was invited
to discuss sports on a radio broadcast. In commenting about
the school's football team, the old man said, 'Our nigger
boys get along well with our white boys.' At this point, the
broadcaster announced, 'Cut, we can't air that.'

Dr. Gini didn't stop there. Ms. Westmoreland relates:

As I sat at my desk, waiting to take more notes, I watched
Dr. Gini pace in front of the class. Suddenly, he stopped
behind the lectern, extended his right arm at full length,
pointed at me and shouted, 'This is a nigger student. We
have a nigger student in our class.' He repeated this
statement several times without lowering the volume of his
voice.
    I was totally shocked. Dr. Gini made me feel as if I
didn't belong in the class. I felt like I had squirmed into the
classroom like an insect that could be stomped on at any
moment. I wanted to run, but I was afraid I would not have
the strength to make it to the door. I feared that if he called
me a nigger one more time, my body would go into a
convulsion.
    When he concluded, I noticed that the class room was
uncharacteristically silent. There wasn't a cough, a
movement of heads, the turning of a page or the motion of
a pen.

Two days later, on January 24, Dr. Gini was describing yuppies, puppies and muppies. When he said, 'Buppies,' he singled me out: 'The young lady sitting in the back of the room is a buppy, a Black urban professional.' Naturally, I felt very uncomfortable again.

On January 26, class met for the last time that week. I remember worrying through the whole period whether I would be used as some kind of example again. I was so nervous from not knowing what to expect that I couldn't concentrate. I knew I couldn't continue in this state and decided to ask Dr. Gini if I could speak to him. I didn't have the courage to speak to him that day, so I waited until the following week.

I didn't attend class on Monday, but I sought out Dr. Gini and asked if he would see me in his office at 12:30 p.m. 'Is there a problem?' he asked jokingly? I said there was. 'Twelve thirty is fine,' he agreed.

I began our appointment by asking the professor if he would please not use me as an example in class. He interrupted: 'I thought this was the reason you wanted to see me.' He continued to say that he had used me as an example on just two occasions, and was very sorry if he embarrassed or offended me. He said he would never do it again. Dr. Gini also added that he uses real examples to demonstrate so that 'they' (the students) can understand his points. Visualization, he told me, helps 'them' to understand more readily.

But what about me? I wondered. I'm also an accredited student who pays tuition. When do I get the opportunity to learn and receive some understanding and enrichment?

After I left Dr. Gini's office, I was even more distraught. I fully recognized that he was not racially empathetic enough for me to receive reinforcement or develop rapport in his class.

Those experiences have made my life very difficult. I can't concentrate on my other courses without thinking about what happened in his class. I even find it difficult to get to sleep at night. I'm looking forward to the day when I can put this episode behind me. But the one thing I know for certain is that this is something I will never forget.

Ms. Westmoreland, a resident of North Lawndale on the West Side of Chicago, felt that there was no hope in trying to get help from the Loyola administration. So she approached Operation PUSH, an organization founded by Rev. Jesse Louis Jackson, which arranged for her to tell her story on radio station WGCI (1390 AM). She concluded the broadcast by appealing for assistance in overcoming the obstacles to continuing her formal education.

Rep. Cardiss Collins, D-7th Congressional District, immediately responded. She promised to investigate the incident and verify whether the school receives federal funds. PUSH national executive director Rev. Tyrone Crider asked for a meeting with school officials. Ald. William C. Henry (24th), said, "The professor has to go."

Chenelle Winters, co-chair of the Black Cultural Center at Loyola University, called for disciplinary action against Professor Gini. "Things are said where the faculty member may not be aware of the impact of what he is saying," she said. "There's a kind of use of hurtful words that can cause pain."

Dr. Kathleen McCourt, acting dean of the Loyola College of Arts and Sciences, defended Dr. Gini: "The professor has apologized for the name calling. He was not aware of the extent of the distress he had caused." Dr. McCourt said the professor denied that he called the coed a nigger student. He did acknowledge that he used racial and ethnic epithets in order to demonstrate how language patterns change over time, she said. His point was not to condone such language but to exemplify that such language has become unacceptable.

"I honestly believe that Dr. Gini thought his behavior was benign; more than that, I believe his efforts were intended to sensitize the class to the ethical inappropriateness of racist language," Dr. McCourt stated.

Dr. McCourt said she did not inform Ms. Westmoreland of her right to file an official grievance because Dr. Gini did not intend for his remarks to be offensive.

"My point was to deny that position," Dr. Gini asserted. "I was arguing against such racism, against such bigots. If I erred, it is because I didn't know that student well enough."

"The 'N' word is the most vile in the English language because it strips people of their humanity, of their dignity," Dr. Gini said. He said he had approached "well over a dozen of my former students" who had been used as examples in other classes and denied that they had been offended.

The professor apologized to Sandra Westmoreland privately, but the leaders of the Black Cultural Center wanted him to issue a public statement. Dr. Gini complied: "I deeply regret that one student in the class misinterpreted the context of my comments. To the best of my knowledge, none of the Black students in my other classes nor any of my other students misunderstood the meaning and purpose of my remarks. In 22 years of teaching, this is the first complaint filed against me for using the 'N' word.

"Nevertheless," Dr. Gini continued, "because the issue is more important than my words, let me once again apologize for offending the sensitivity of the student in question. However, I do not feel that my intentions or purpose were racial or unethical. My point was to deny the word and explain why it was wrong to use it."

No positive intention was ever meant to be derived form the use of the word nigger. The "N" word used in combination with other acts can psychologically destroy a person, as evidenced by Sabrina Collins, an 18-year-old coed at Emory University in Atlanta. Ms. Collins was hospitalized at the Augusta Hospital psychiatric ward after apparently suffering an emotional breakdown as a result of a racist campaign leveled at her.

In the first instance, Ms. Collins' room was ransacked. Her clothes were splattered with bleach and her stuffed animals were ripped apart. The words "nigger hang" were written in her closet. Over a period of five weeks, intruders wrote in her room six more racial epithets and sent her threatening letters before she was hospitalized with an apparent nervous breakdown.

The Georgia Bureau of Investigations, DeKalb County Police, Emory Police and the FBI were investigating the case as of April 20, 1990. Kendall Wood, a sophomore at Emory University, said, "The climate here at Emory is conducive to this type of behavior. It's not an isolated incident."

Racism appears in many guises. Fran McBride, a Black member of the faculty in the School of Journalism at the University of Missouri, Columbia, asked a colleague, Mark Pardee, manager of KOMU, the university's television channel, why more Black people did not appear on the weekly program "People You Should Know."

"Do you know any watermelon salesmen I should know?" Pardee retorted.

Isolation is a thumb of racism that has been imprinted on Black faculty as well as Black students.

Professor Johnnell E. Butler, the first Black woman to gain tenure at Smith College in North Hampton, Mass., resigned after 13 years on the faculty and charged the school with making only perfunctory efforts to combat racism. Two administrators, Gregory Vaughn and Alice Smith, followed suit. Mr. Vaughn said, "As minority administrators, we are not involved in the mainstream when it comes to key decision making." Ms. Smith echoed, "I am isolated from the process of setting policy."

Heather Robinson, a student at the University of Michigan at Ann Arbor, remembers a night in 1987 when a flyer was slipped under the door of a dormitory lounge where some Black women were holding a meeting. The leaflet declared "open hunting season on porch monkeys also known as jigaboos, jungle bunnies and spooks."

Ms. Robinson, a 20-year-old Black resident of Detroit, said she had always felt somewhat unwelcome among the students on the Michigan campus, most of whom were white. After the flyer incident, she said she began to feel withdrawn and afraid. "I know that I am not wanted here, and don't like being here," she complained.

In 1988, Black student enrollment at the University of Michigan represented about 5.7 percent of the student body of 50,000, slightly higher than the 5.6 percent of the previous year. At this rate, it has been observed that the school will not reach its target of 12 percent Black enrollment until the year 2050.

Veronica Woolridge, a Black student at the university, observed, "Programs designed to recruit and retain minority students and faculty seem nothing more than a public relations ploy."

In April of 1989, members of the Michigan faculty voted down a proposal to require students to take a course on ethnicity and racism.

Veronica was indignant: "Education is the key to understanding and respecting individual and cultural differences. The faculty's refusal to adopt a course that would have advanced these goals runs counter to its responsibility to educate its students," she said.

Veronica, a junior with about 80 credit hours, has had only one Black instructor, a visiting professor from Wayne University in Detroit.

Ms. Woolridge notes that Black students at Michigan have a kind of unwritten code:

When we see each other, even if we are not acquainted, we often offer a greeting in support. In most of my classes, some of which have up to 200 students, the few Blacks will sit together, as they do in the cafeteria—an attempt to survive in a white, elite institution.

White students are often even more to blame for separatism. They do not question segregation often enough; they take it for granted. Black and white students seldom interact except by competing academically. Many Michigan students like to show their wealth with cars, clothes and spring vacations.

Competition results in acts of overt racism, like a flyer that circulated last year declaring April 1989 as 'white pride time,' featuring such events as counseling sessions on how to deal with 'uppity niggers.'

Jeff Turner, a student at the University of Georgia, notes that many Black students come from Atlanta's public high school system. The first Negro public high school in the city, Booker T. Washington, was not built until 1924. Today, Black students are the majority in the Atlanta schools. The races don't often meet socially in Georgia—or, indeed, in many parts of America where segregation has been sanctified by custom.

As a group, Blacks make up only 5 percent of the total student population at the University of Georgia, in a state where more than 25 percent of the population is Black. Black students understandably feel out of place. Some say they feel intimidated when they walk into a room and discover they're the only Black in a class of more than a hundred students. The residence halls also reflect separatism. When Blacks choose one dormitory, whites tend to choose any of the others.

In contrast, the dormitories are integrated at the Citadel Military College of South Carolina, Charleston, S.C. But it was at good old "Cit" that five white cadets wearing white sheets over their heads like Ku Klux Klan members left a singed paper cross in the room of a Black freshman.

Leaving burning crosses on the lawns of Blacks is old stuff for college men. Several fraternities at the University of Wisconsin, Madison, in an effort to be creative, held a party featuring a "Harlem room." Watermelon and fried chicken was served in the room, where trash littered the floor and graffiti decorated the wall. Members of the fraternity wore Afro wigs and Black-face make up. In an effort to out do the Kappa Sigma Fraternity, the Phi Gamma Delta Fraternity held a "Figi Island" party that displayed a caricature of a Black man with a bone through his nose. In the fall of 1988, the Zeta Beta Tau Fraternity held a mock slave auction in which members wore Afro wigs and Black face during several skits.

Each incident provoked outrage from the Madison campus and community: large demonstrations were held outside the fraternity houses and sentiment mounted for the abolition of fraternities and sororities.

The Justice Department Community Relations Service estimates that campus racial incidents rose to 96 in 1989 from 34 in fiscal 1987, when the department began its racial tally on college activities.

From October 31, 1989, through January 31, 1990, 28 incidents of racial disturbances erupted on American campuses. In February 1990, a portrait of the late Mayor Harold Washington, which hangs in a place of honor at Northwestern University's Law School, Chicago, was defaced. The same month, students at Vassar College, Poughkeepsie, N.Y., demanded that Sen. Daniel Patrick Moynihan (D-New York) be stripped of the prestigious Eleanor Roosevelt chair for an alleged racist remark. Folami Gray, a Jamaican who is the executive director of the Duchess County Youth Bureau, said Sen. Moynihan had insulted her when she disagreed with his argument that America was a model of ethnic cooperation. "He responded to me by saying I can pack my bags and return to where I came from."

At the New York University Law School, a brochure describing a law conference for minority women was defaced by adding the phrases "you know who" and signed by "students of European descent." Other incidents have scarred the law school. A laundry ticket was tacked to the bulletin board of an Asian student group. A poster of Jesse Jackson was ripped from the door of a dormitory room occupied by a Hispanic woman. When she hung it up again, someone set it on fire.

Foebe Eng, a third-year student, said, "The fact that people find an atmosphere that might not sanction these incidents but allows them to go on says a lot."

In the spring of '89, three of the 70 faculty members at the law school were minorities. Dean John Sexton, who demands that efforts be made to attract minority faculty, said that five minority persons would be invited to join the faculty in the 1991 academic year.

Seventeen percent of the students at the New York Law School are minorities. This is higher than the national average of 11 percent, though students claim that NYU ranks ninth among the top 10 law schools in the percentage of minority students and faculty.

Many in campus communities believe that a larger minority population would encourage positive interaction that could deflate incentives for racism and nourish sensitivity among both students and faculties. A renewed spirit would replace reactionary rhetoric environments with realistic educational opportunities.

The administration at the University of Mississippi certainly needed sensitivity when the first Black cheerleader at the university refused to follow the custom of carrying the Confederate flag at a football game. The school responded to growing protests from students of both races by announcing that the Confederate flag would no longer serve as the school's traditional symbol. The following year, the "Ole Miss" yearbook carried pictures of the Ku Klux Klan carrying a Confederate flag as well as photos of the Black protests that led to its demise.

In contrast, a yearbook produced by the Black Student League of the University of Pennsylvania, Philadelphia, comprises photographs and articles that depict positive aspects of Black awareness.

"The 128-page yearbook was created after the group decided it needed an outlet to reflect Black achievements and the role of Blacks on campus because other publications had failed to recognize them fairly," said Terry White, the project faculty advisor. Professor White thinks that "Positive Black" is the first such publication at an Ivy League institution.

"Positive Black," which was distributed in the spring of 1989, resembles most college annuals in all aspects but one: it portrays only Black faculty, undergraduates and clubs, including the Black Pen Arts League and the Black Wharton Undergraduate Association.

"Given the environment of our campus, I think the Blacks need something like this," Ms. White said. "From outside, viewing our official publication, you would think that there were just one or two Black students on campus."

Positive attitudes, like those that launched and supported the alternative yearbook at Pennsylvania, often are born and nourished in the home. But as the song from the 1949 Broadway production "South Pacific," featuring Mary Martin, shows, "You have to be taught... to be carefully taught to hate."

Comedian Bill Cosby, whose charitable donations include gifts of millions of dollars to several American universities and colleges, almost literally ran into a sample of this kind of teaching.

According to a story that appeared in the April 4, 1990, issue of *Jet* magazine, Cosby was jogging on the University of Las Vegas track, when a white family—four children and their father—approached him. The 4-year-old daughter told Cosby that she loved his TV show, but her mother will not watch it because she hates Black people. Cosby and the little girl's father were shocked by the disclosure. Cosby said, "I'm looking at the child, who's being told by the first messenger that she hates a certain kind of people, a certain color of people . . . and I looked at the father and the father was stunned. 'That's quite an interesting home you have'," I told him.

If racism is taught to babies by the mothers, who are the children's first messengers, how can we expect the teenager entering the university to be civil and respectful of others of a different culture and skin tone?

In *Souls of Black Folk*, written in 1903, Dr. W.E.B. DuBois predicted that the problem of the 20th century would be the color line. Dr. DuBois died June 27, 1963, at age 95 in Accra, Ghana, where he had lived for some years in self-imposed exile because America had failed to live up to the principles of the 14th and 15th amendments to the constitution.

Twenty-six days before the death of Dr. DuBois, two Black students, escorted by National Guard troops and other federal officials, enrolled at the University of Alabama, Tuscaloosa, despite the opposition of Gov. George C. Wallace.

Medgar W. Evers, 37, NAACP field secretary of Mississippi, was assassinated in front of his Jackson home 15 days before Dr. DuBois' demise. Thirty-two days after the death of Dr. Dubois, Dr. Martin Luther King Jr. led the civil rights march in Washington, D.C., where more than 250,000 people heard him deliver his stirring "I Have A Dream" address. Five months after W.E.B. DuBois' death, John F. Kennedy, the 35th president of the United States, who at age 46 believed that he could recreate a Camelot, was assassinated in Dallas on November 22, 1963.

W.E.B. DuBois' prediction of the color line will hold as true for the 21st century as it has for the 20th century. Negating DuBois' prophecy could be aided by making it mandatory to teach courses in the history of racism in America to elementary, high school and university students as a requirement for graduation. If Dick and Jane readers, European history and gym classes are compulsory, there is no reason for the racial history of America to be excluded from educational programs.

It is paramount that we learn to live with each other in this country. America can survive only as one nation, indivisible. If we continue as two nations, one Black and one white, separate and unequal, we will expend our energies on the borders of hate and lose the intelligence, courage and strength to create a land of true opportunity where understanding and cooperation are the watch words.

BIBLIOGRAPHY

BOOKS

Adams, Russell L., *Great Negroes Past and Present*, Chicago: Afro-Am Publishing Co., 1963.

African Past to the Civil War, By the Editors of Ebony, Ebony Pictorial History of Black America Vol. I, Chicago: Johnson Publishing Co. Inc., 1971.

Allen, A.B., *Toward Fair Employment and the EEOC: A Study for Compliance with Title VII of the Civil Rights Act of 1969*, Washington, D.C.: U.S. Equal Employment Opportunity Commission, 1972.

Allen, R.L., *Black Awakening in Capitalist America: An Analytical History*, Garden City, N.Y.: Doubleday, 1970.

America, Richard F. and Bernard E. Anderson, *Moving Ahead: Black Managers in American Business*, New York: McGraw-Hill Inc., 1978.

Anderson, Jervis, *This was Harlem: A Cultural Portrait, 1900-1915*, New York: Farrar, Straus & Giroux Inc., 1982.

Ashe, Arthur R. Jr., *A Hard Road to Glory: A History of the African-American Athlete 1619-1918*, New York: Warner Books Inc., 1988.

Ashe, Arthur R. Jr., *A Hard Road to Glory: A History of the African-American Athlete 1919-1945*, New York: Warner Books Inc., 1988.

Ashe, Arthur R. Jr., *A Hard Road to Glory: A History of the African-American Athlete 1946*, New York: Warner Books Inc., 1988.

Bennett, Lerone Jr., *The Challenge of Blackness*, Chicago: Johnson Publishing Co. Inc., 1972.

Blumrosen, Alfred W., *Black Employment and the Law*, New Brunswick, N.J.: Rutgers University Press, 1971.

Calloway, Cab, and Bryant Rollins, *Of Minnie the Moocher and Me*, New York: Thomas Y. Crowell Co., 1976.

Chicago Schools: Worst in America, Chicago: The Chicago Tribune Co., 1988.

Civil Rights Movement to Black Revolution, By the Editors of Ebony, Ebony Pictorial History of Black America Vol. III, Chicago: Johnson Publishing Co. Inc., 1971.

Cleaver, Eldridge, *Soul on Ice*, New York: McGraw-Hill Inc., 1968.

Cohen, Peter, *The Gospel According to the Harvard Business School*, New York: Penguin USA, 1973.

Cohn, Jules, *The Conscience of Corporations: Business and Urban Affairs, 1967-1970*, Baltimore, Md.: The John Hopkins University Press, 1971.

Commager, Henry Steele, *The Struggle for Racial Equality*, New York: Harper & Row Publishers

Inc., 1951.

Cox, Allan, *Inside Corporate America*, New York: St. Martin's Press Inc., 1982.

Cripps, Thomas, *Slow Fade to Black— The Negro in American Film, 1900-1942*, New York: Oxford University Press Inc., 1977.

Davis, George and Glegg Watson, *Black Life in Corporate America; Swimming in the Mainstream*, Garden City, N.Y.: Anchor Press-Doubleday, 1982.

Detweiler, Frederick, *The Negro Press in the United States*, Chicago: The University of Chicago Press, 1972.

Dickens Jr., Floyd and Jacqueline B. Dickens, *The Black Manager, Making it in the Corporate World*, New York: AMACOM Book Division (American Management Association), 1982.

Doob, Leonard W., *Public Opinion and Propaganda*, Hamden, Conn.: Archon Books, 1966.

Dornfeld, A.A., *Behind the Front; Page The Story of the City News Bureau of Chicago*, Chicago: Academy Chicago Publishers, 1983.

Drake, St. Clair and Horace Cayton, *Black Metropolis—A Study of Negro Life in the Northern City*, Vols. I and II, New York: Harper & Row Publishers Inc., 1945.

DuBois, W.E.B. *Souls of Black Folk*, Chicago: McClurg Publishers, 1903.

Ehrenreich, Barbara, *Fear of Falling; The End of Life of the Middle Class*, New York: Pantheon Books Inc., 1989.

Ewing, Davis, ed., *American Popular Songs From the Revolutionary War to the Present*, New York: Random House Inc., 1966.

Famous Blacks Give Secret of Success, By the Editors of Ebony, Ebony Success Library: Vol. II, Chicago:

Johnson Publishing Co. Inc., 1973.

Floyd, Thomas W., *Integration is a Bitch*, Gary, Ind.: Tom Floyd's Visuals Inc., 1969.

Frazier, E. Franklin, *The Black Bourgeoisie: The Rise of a New Middle Class*, New York: The Free Press, 1964.

Frederickson, George M., *The Black Image in the White Mind*, New York: Harper & Row Publishers Inc., 1971.

Gelber, Steven M., *Black Men and Business Men; The Growing Awareness of Social Responsibility*, Port Washington, N.Y.: Kennikat Press, 1974.

Giddings, Paula, *When and Where I Enter The Impact of Black Women on Race and Sex in America*, New York: Bantam Books, 1984.

Glazier, Nathan and Daniel Patrick Moynihan, *Beyond the Melting Pot*, Cambridge, Mass.: Massachusetts Institute of Technology, 1963.

Grier, William H. and Price M. Cobbs, *Black Rage*, New York: Basic Books Inc., Publishers, 1968.

Griffith, Richard and Arthur Mayer. *The Movies*, New York: Simon and Schuster Inc., 1970.

Harris, Abram L., *The Negro As A Capitalist: A Study of Banking and Business Among American Negroes*, Philadelphia: American Academy of Political and Social Science, 1936.

Haskins, Jim, *The Cotton Club*, New York: Random House Inc., 1977.

Jaynes, Gerald David and Robert M. Williams Jr. eds., *A Common Destiny: Blacks and American Society*, Washington, D.C.: National Academy Press, 1989.

Johnson, James Weldon, *The Autobiography of an Ex-Coloured*

Man; The Vivid Story of a Negro Who Crossed the Color Line, New York: Alfred A. Knopf Inc., 1912.

Johnson, John H. with Lerone Bennett Jr., *Succeeding Against the Odds*, New York: Warner Books Inc., 1989.

Katzman, David M., Mary Beth Norton, Paul D. Escat, Howard P. Chudacoff, Thomas G. Patterson and William Tuttle Jr., *A People and A Nation—A History of the United States*, Boston: Houghton Mifflin Co., 1982.

Lacy, Leslie Alexander, *The Rise and Fall of A Proper Negro: An Autobiography of Leslie Alexander Lacy*, MacMillan Publishers Co., 1970.

Lait, Jack and Lee Mortimer, *New York: Confidential*, Chicago: Sziff-Davidson Publishing Co., 1948.

Landry, Bart, *The New Black Middle Class*, Berkeley, Calif.: University of California Press, 1987.

Lee, Ulysses, *United States Army and World War II Special Studies: The Employment of Negro Troops*, Washington, D.C.: Office of the Chief of Military History, United States Army, 1966.

Lewis David Lavering, *When Harlem was in Vogue*, New York: Alfred A. Knopf Inc., 1981.

Lockwood, Charles, *Manhattan Moves Uptown*, Boston: Houghton Mifflin Co., 1976.

Lomax, Louis, *The Negro Revolt*, New York: Signet Books, 1963.

MacDonald, J. Fred, *Black and White TV—Afro-Americans in Television Since 1948*, Chicago: Nelson-Hall Publishers, 1983.

MacDonald, J. Fred, *Don't Touch that Dial!—Radio Programming and American Life, 1920-1960*, Chicago: Nelson-Hall Publishers, 1979.

Mays, Benjamin E. *Born to Rebel: An Autobiography of Benjamin E. Mays*, New York: Charles Scribner & Sons, 1971.

McKay, Claude, *Harlem: A Negro Metropolis*, New York: E.P. Dutton & Co. Inc., 1940.

Monsen, R. Joseph, *Business and the Changing Environment*, New York: McGraw-Hill Inc., 1973.

Newman, Mark, *Entrepreneurs of Profit and Pride—From Black Appeal to Radio Soul*, New York: Praeger Publishers, 1988.

The 1973 Yearbook, By the Editors of Ebony, Ebony Pictorial History of Black America Vol. IV, Chicago: Johnson Publishing Co. Inc., 1973.

Ofari, Earl, *The Myth of Black Capitalism*, New York: Monthly Review Press, 1970.

1000 Successful Blacks, By the Editors of Ebony, Ebony Success Library: Vol. I, Chicago: Johnson Publishing Co. Inc., 1973.

Osofsky, Gilbert, *Harlem: The Making of a Ghetto Negro New York 1890-1930*, New York: Harper & Row Publishers Inc., 1965.

Ottley, Roi, *The Lonely Warrior—The Life and Times of Robert S. Abbott*, Chicago: Henry Regnery, 1955.

Packard, Vance, *The Status Seekers; An Exploration of Class Behavior in America and the Hidden Barriers that Affect You, the Community, Your Future*, New York: David McKay Co. Inc., 1959.

Peters, Thomas J. and Robert H. Waterman Jr., *In Search of Excellence; Lessons from America's Best Run Companies*, New York: Harper & Row Publishers Inc., 1982.

Powell, Adam Clayton, *Adam by*

Adam: The Autobiography of Adam Clayton Powell, New York: Dial Press, 1971.

Reconstruction to Supreme Court Decision 1952, By the Editors of Ebony, Ebony Pictorial History of Black America Vol. II, Chicago: Johnson Publishing Co. Inc., 1971.

Robinson, Jackie as told to Alfred Duckett, I Never Had it Made, New York: G.P. Putnam Sons, 1972.

Rose, Arnold M. (ed.), *Race, Prejudice and Discrimination*, New York: Alfred A. Knopf Inc., 1953.

Rosen, N.S., (ed.), *Studies in Labor Markets*, Chicago: University of Chicago Press, 1981.

Schiffman, Jack, *Uptown: The Story of Harlem's Apollo Theater*, New York: Coles Book Co. Inc., 1971.

Schoener, Alan, ed. *Harlem on My Mind; The Cultural Capital of Black America 1900-1968*, New York: Random House Inc., 1960.

Scott Blue Book 1957; Business and Service Directory of Greater Chicago, Chicago, Ill., 1947.

Seder, John and Berkley G. Burrell, *Getting It Together; Black Businessmen in America*, New York: Harcourt Brace Jovanovich Inc., 1971.

Silberman, Charles E., *Crisis in Black and White*, New York: Random House Inc., 1964.

Simms' Blue Book and National Negro Business and Professional Directory, compiled by James N. Simms, Chicago: James N. Simms, 1923.

Sowell, Thomas, *Ethnic America*, New York: Basic Books Inc., Publishers, 1981.

Sowell, Thomas, *Race and Economics*, New York: Longman Inc., 1975.

Stein, M.L., *Shaping the News: The Media's Function in Today's World*, New York: Washington Square Press, 1974.

Strickland, Arbarh E., *History of the Chicago Urban League*, Champaign, Ill.: University of Illinois Press, 1966.

Terkel, Studs, *Division Street America*, New York: Pantheon Books Inc., 1967.

Terkel, Studs, *The Good War: An Oral History of World War II*, New York: Pantheon Books Inc., 1984.

Travis, Dempsey J., *An Autobiography of Black Chicago*, Chicago: Urban Research Institute, 1981.

Travis, Dempsey J., *An Autobiography of Black Jazz*, Chicago: Urban Research Press, 1983.

Travis, Dempsey J., *An Autobiography of Black Politics*, Chicago: Urban Research Press, 1987.

Tuleja, Tad, *Beyond the Bottom Line: How Business Leaders are Turning Principles into Profit*, New York: Penguin USA, 1985.

van Vechtene, Karl, *Nigger Heaven*, New York: Alfred A. Knopf Inc., 1926.

Warner, W. Lloyd, *Social Class in America; The Evaluation of Status*, New York: Harper & Row Publishers Inc., 1960.

Waters, Enoc P., *American Diary—A Personal History of the Black Press*, Chicago: Path Press Inc., 1987.

Who's Who Among Black Americans 1975-1976, Vol. I.: Who's Who Among Black Americans Inc., Northbrook, Ill., 1976.

Who's Who in America, 44th edition 1988-89, Vol. 2.: Marquis Who's

Who, Wilmette, Ill., 1989.

Yette, Samuel F., *A Choice—The Issue of Black Discrimination in America*, New York: Berkley Publishing Group, 1975.

MAGAZINES

"Black Face, Hollywood Style," *Negro Digest*, February 1944.

"Who Wants to be White?," *Negro Digest*, December 1, 1949.

"Is Intermarriage Wrecking the NAACP?," *Negro Digest*, June 1, 1950.

"I Passed for a Negro," *Negro Digest*, June 1, 1950.

"Black No More," *Negro Digest*, April 1, 1950

"I'm Through With Passing," *Ebony*, March 1951.

"Thousands Live Jekyl-Hyde Existence to Hold Down Jobs," *Ebony*, April 1952.

"What Happened to 'Lost Boundaries' Family," *Ebony*, August 1952.

"I Passed for Negro," *Our World*, August 1, 1953.

"Curse of Passing," *Ebony*, December 1955.

"Time to Grow Up," *Ebony*, February 1956.

"Passed for White," *Ebony*, April 1957.

"Man Who Chose Loneliness," *Ebony*, May 1958

"New Bias Laws Speed Louisiana Integration," *Ebony*, May 1958.

"I Lived Two Lives for 30 Years," *Ebony*, June 1959.

"Rooms for Miracles," *American Education*, August/September 1969.

"To Live in Harlem," *National Geographic*, February 1977.

"TV Newscasters," *Ebony*, January 1979.

"Blaxploitation in the Media," *Message*, September 1981.

"Manhattan-Images of the City," *National Geographic*, September 1981.

"Brooklyn: The Other Side of the Bridge," *National Geographic*, May 1983.

"The Dream Deferred," *Harvard Business Review*, May-June 1986.

"TV Station Boycotted by PUSH Hires Black Anchor," *Jet*, August 11, 1986.

"Network to Network," *Black Enterprise*, February 1987.

"Journalists Win Bias Suit," *Black Enterprise*, July 1987.

"Blacks in Sports 40 Years After Robinson," *The Crisis*, November 1987.

"The Doug Williams Story," *U.S. Sports*, February 1988.

"Dead Max Robinson 49," *Time*, January 2, 1989.

"Max Robinson: Fighting the Demons," *Newsweek*, January 2, 1989.

"His Brother's Keeper," *Jet*, January 9, 1989.

"New Racism on Campus," *Fortune*, February 13, 1989.

"Racism Ingrained in U.S. Culture Says Activist Alvin Poussaint," *AIM*, Fall 1989.

"Closing the Gate on Talent," *The Quill*, October 1989.

"Forty Under Forty," *Crain's Chicago Business*, October 9, 1989.

"The Boston Murder: Race, Anger and a Divided City." *Newsweek*, January 22, 1990.

"A Murderous Hoax," *Newsweek*, January 22, 1990.

"Raised Hope in a Divided City," *Newsweek*, January 22, 1990.

"Black Studies Pioneer, Ewart Juinier,

79, Dies," *Jet*, February 26, 1990.

"Harvard Review Gets First Black President," *Jet*, February 26, 1990.

"Who's Black and Who's Not?," *Ebony*, March 1990.

"The Academy snubs 'Do The Right Thing' and embraces 'Driving Miss Daisy' What's wrong with Oscar?" *Entertainment Magazine*, 19 March 1990.

"Cosby Chastises White Parent for Teaching Her Children to Hate Blacks," *Jet*, April 2, 1990.

"Emory Students Protest Racial Harassment that Led to Coed's Breakdown," *Jet*, April 30, 1990.

NEWSPAPERS

1965-1969

"The Challenge of Ray School," *Hyde Park Herald*, August 1965.

"Ask Federal Funds for Ray School Experimental Learning Center," *Hyde Park Herald*, 17 January 1968.

"Key School Unit Names its First Negro Member," *Chicago Daily News*, 15 February 1968.

"Can Pupil Transfer Help? Here's Proof it Does," *Chicago Daily News*, 29 February 1968.

"Ray Principal Heads Up New Challenge," *Chicago Sun-Times*, 4 March 1968.

"New Principal at Ray School," *Ray News*, 19 March 1968.

"First Negro On Examining Unit," *Chicago Daily News*, 27 June 1968.

"Chathamite is School Board First Black Appointment to Certification Post," *The Bulletin*, 3 July 1968.

"Teacher's Pact Will Change Hiring Policy," *Chicago Tribune*, 1 June 1969.

1970-1979

"Do people attempt to repeat history?," *Chicago Tribune*, 3 December 1972.

"Old Black Joe is dead. Hurrah!" *Chicago Tribune Magazine*, 3 December 1972.

"Deprived Ones are Often Affected," *Chicago Defender*, 4 August 1977.

1980-1989

"The Black plight: race or class," *The New York Times Magazine*, 5 October 1980.

"Robinson of ABC News quoted as saying networks discriminate," *The New York Times*, 11 February 1981.

"Destroying Black self-image," *Chicago Defender*, 8 August 1981.

"The insidious new racism," *Chicago Tribune*, 31 August 1981.

"Racism: Early childhood causes," *Chicago Defender*, 5 September 1981.

"What happened to blacks?" *Chicago Defender*, 17 October 1981.

"Tony Brown's Journal endures," *The New York Times*, 7 February 1982.

"Taking a chance: Many Blacks jump off the corporate ladder to be entrepreneurs," *Wall Street Journal*, 2 August 1984.

"Lawmakers enter U of I bias dispute," *Chicago Defender*, 20 March 1985.

"Black professionals refashion their careers," *The New York Times*, 29 November 1985.

"A shifting in images: Race, sex and TV news," *Chicago Tribune Magazine*, 13 July 1986.

"The ax falls on equal opportunity," *The New York Times*, 4 January 1987.

"Claim racism among Blacks still exists," *Chicago Defender*, 27

March 1987.

"Ole Miss...'desgregated by not integrated,'" *Chicago Defender*, 14 April 1987.

"Daily News found guilty in bias suit," *Chicago Defender*, 18 April 1987.

"Aurora racial tension builds," *Chicago Defender*, 18 April 1987.

"College sees racism grow with campus," *Chicago Tribune*, 21 April 1987.

"Anchorman wins bias suit," *Pittsburgh Courier*, 2 May 1987.

"NIU changes bylaws to deal with bias," *Chicago Defender*, 3 May 1987.

"Bias is charged at Missouri U.," *The New York Times*, 4 May 1987.

"Chicago's two major dailies at standstill," *Chicago Reporter*, 12 May 1987.

"Georgia U. properly handled incident," *Chicago Defender*, 20 June 1987.

"Atlanta schools among nation's most segregated," *Chicago Defender*, 23 July 1987.

"Buckwheat craze was bad enough the first time," *Chicago Defender* August 26, 1987.

"Women still lagging in key TV jobs," *Chicago Sun-Times*, 30 August 1987.

"Even before the coffee—AM News Anchor Middlebrooks has loyal following," *Skyline*, 14 September 1987.

"Blacks can't be barred in racial trial," *Chicago Defender*, 24 September 1987.

"NIU trying to break new bigotry barriers," *Chicago Tribune*, 4 October 1987.

"Court upset with findings of Alabama college bias," *Chicago Sun-Times*, 7 October 1987.

"Howard beach attorneys address jury," *The New York Times*, 8 October 1987.

"University racism," *Chicago Defender*, 22 October 1987.

"Three Howard Beach teens guilty," *Chicago Sun-Times*, 22 December 1987.

"Howard Beach black jury flap continues," *Chicago Defender*, 23 December 1987.

"Howard Beach verdict mixed: Residents unsure neighborhood will be absolved," *Chicago Tribune*, 23 December 1987.

"Howard Beach verdict sensible, but case may have to be tried," *Chicago Sun-Times*, 26 December 1987.

"All-Male clubs at Harvard assailed for bias," *The New York Times*, 29 December 1987.

"Study finds integration slow for Blacks," *Chicago Tribune*, 30 December 1987.

"3 at Smith assert neglect of Blacks," *The New York Times*, 30 December 1987.

"Turmoil at Ohio State in shunning of student," *The New York Times*, 31 January 1988.

"Probe launched into alleged college racism," *Chicago Defender*, 6 February 1988.

"Black studies out last their critics," *Chicago Tribune*, 14 February 1988.

"Blacks skip college at rising rate," *Chicago Tribune*, 22 February 1988.

"Hampshire College students protest racism at school," *Chicago Defender*, 25 February 1988.

"Hampshire students vow to continue studying," *Chicago Defender*, 27 February 1988.

"Campus confab on racism seen as first step," *Chicago Defender*, 9 March 1988.

"Is racism on campus increasing?"
Chicago Tribune, 13 March 1988.

"Penn State worries arrest may hurt
minority efforts," *The New York
Times*, 20 April 1988.

"Campus battle pits freedom of speech
against racial slurs," *The New
York Times*, 25 April 1988.

"Campus racism is rampant in U.S.,"
Chicago Defender, 27 April 1988.

"Gannett surpasses other newspaper
firms," *Wall Street Journal*, 11 May
1988.

"Exploring the roots of campus
racism," *Chicago Sun-Times*, 3
June 1988.

"New coalition elected at U. of Mass.,"
The New York Times, 22 June
1988.

"Japanese puzzled by charges of
racism for black stereotypes,"
Chicago Tribune, 28 August 1988.

"Study links subtle sex bias in schools
with women's behavior in the
workplace," *The New York Times*,
16 September 1988.

"BALSA case raises question of a
misuse of minority hiring," *The
New York Times*, 9 October 1988.

"Prejudice on campuses feared to be
rising," *The New York Times*, 31
October 1988.

"Max Robinson, First Black to anchor
network news," *Chicago Tribune*,
21 December 1988.

"Tough job of teaching ethics," *The
New York Times*, 22 January 1989.

"U of C may ban law firm's
recruiting," *Chicago Sun-Times*, 2
February 1989.

"U. of Chgo Bars recruiters of top
firm," *The New York Times*, 3
February 1989.

"Ranks of Black Men Shrink on US
campuses," *The New York Times*,
5 February 1989.

"As Oakland rises, its paper endures,"

The New York Times, 6 February
1989.

"Students at NYU protest race bias,"
New York Times, March 3, 1989.

"Howard Univ. president threatens to
arrest students," *The New York
Times*, 9 March 1989.

"Protests at Howard U. bring surprise
review," *The New York Times*, 16
March 1989.

"Race reaction on campus," *The New
York Times*, 5 April 1989.

"Making their mark on the press,"
Chicago Sun-Times, 23 April 1989.

"In rift at Cornell, racial issues of 60's
resurface," *The New York Times*,
3 May 1989.

"Muzzle the Stanford bigots," *The
New York Times*, 12 May 1989.

"55 arrested in Stanford racism
protest," *Tribune*, 16 May 1989.

"Campus racial strains show two
perspectives," *The New York
Times*, 22 May 1989.

"Racist acts inspire a call for control
over fraternities," *The New York
Times*, 22 May 1989.

"School reaches out to Blacks," *The
New York Times*, 24 May 1989.

"Michigan U. is sued over anti-bias
policy," *The New York Times*, 27
May 1989.

"Many families cross color lines to
real world," *The New York Times*,
10 June 1989.

"Tribune's N.Y. newspaper settles
discrimination suit," *Chicago
Tribune*, 12 June 1989.

"Laying bare the bias in the press,"
Chicago Defender, 20 June 1989.

"Racial bias causes college nightmare,"
Chicago Sun-Times, 28 June 1989.

"A rich explanation of HUD scandal,"
Chicago Tribune, 13 July 1989.

"U.S. Black bishop rebuffs priest,"
Chicago Tribune, 13 July 1989.

"Concordia College hit for unfairness,"

Chicago Defender, 13 July 1989.

"No guts no glory for corporate advertisers," *Chicago Sun-Times*, 19 July 1989.

"Black students get a yearbook of their own," *The New York Times*, 21 July 1989.

"U of C study cites 'hypersegregation,'" *Chicago Defender*, 9 August 1989.

"Black liberation radio shut down," *Pittsburgh Courier*, 12 August 1989.

"Black journalists seeking new gains in the newsroom," *The New York Times*, 17 August 1989.

"How Black should a Black journalist be?," *Chicago Sun-Times*, 20 August 1989.

"Sense of muscle for Black journalists," *The New York Times*, 21 August 1989.

"Hispanics hit television bias," *Chicago Defender*, 2 September 1989.

"Study says TV avoids racial conflict, *Pittsburgh Courier*, 2 September 1989.

"Miss America, a serene queen," *USA Today*, 18 September 1989.

"Missouri student crowned Miss America," *The New York Times*, 18 September 1989.

"Blacks can be anti-Black too," *Chicago Sun-Times*, 21 September 1989.

"Fraternity apologizes for racial incident," *Chicago Tribune*, 21 September 1989.

"Miss America snub: Media racist, sexist?," *USA Today*, 22 September 1989.

"Mixed-race generation emerges but is not sure," *The New York Times*, 24 September 1989.

"For Black director, message survives financial realities," *Chicago Tribune*, 25 September 1989.

"Lack of contact blamed for racial tension here," *Chicago Sun-Times*, 28 September 1989.

"Jackie Mason jars New York with remarks on Blacks," *Chicago Sun-Times*, 29 September 1989.

"Segregation holds back Blacks here: Task force," *Chicago Sun-Times*, 29 September 1989.

"Apparent rise in bias crimes may lead to wreckage law," *Chicago Tribune*, 1 October 1989.

"Stagflation for female engineers," *The New York Times*, 1 October 1989.

"Comedian Mason's unfunny remarks help David Dinkins," *Chicago Tribune*, 2 October 1989.

"Someone should study how racist language affects us," *Chicago Sun-Times*, 3 October 1989.

"Former Reagan aide for HUD denies pushing housing projects," *The New York Times*, 3 October 1989.

"Racial study describes pressing problem," *The Hyde Park Herald*, 4 October 1989.

"New York's race has its Willie Horton too," *Chicago Tribune*, 4 October 1989.

"Ex-employee levels racial discrimination charges on temporary employment agency," *Pittsburgh Courier*, 6 October 1989.

"Blacks in sports need affirmative action," *USA Today*, 6 October 1989.

"Blacks in sports are getting fair play," *USA Today*, 6 October 1989.

"Agents say Black players blocked by glass ceiling," *USA Today*, 6 October 1989.

"News people don't need pretty faces," *USA Today*, 6 October 1989.

"Author says media afraid of Jackson book," *Pittsburgh Courier*, 7 October 1989.

"Inside Japan, but always an outsider," *The New York Times*, 7 October 1989.

"The race issue won't die in November," *The New York Times*, 7 October 1989.

"It's a Black thing that networks don't understand," *The Crusader*, 7 October 1989.

"Pay equity for women's jobs find success outside courts," *The New York Times*, 7 October 1989.

"Japan action in World War II: Debate on censorship is renewed," *The New York Times*, 8 October 1989.

"What students think: Racism is big issue," *The New York Times*, 9 October 1989.

"Immunity is considered for two HUD witnesses," *The New York Times*, 9 October 1989.

"Boston Agonizes Over Growing Street Violence," *The New York Times*, 28 October 1989.

"Adam Clayton Powell: The American Experience," *Chicago Defender*, 18 November 1989.

"A Haunted Hero: WTTW documentary unveils life of Adam Clayton Powell," *Chicago Tribune*, 29 November 1989.

1990

"Husband of slain Boston woman becomes a suspect, then a suicide," *The New York Times*, 5 January 1990.

"Boston case: What went wrong?" *The New York Times*, 6 January 1990.

"Murder hoax angers Boston Blacks; Rip "lynching" attitude in Stuart case," *Chicago Sun-Times*, 6 January 1990.

"The verdict on Marshall," *Chicago Sun-Times*, 7 January 1990.

"Boston in uproar over murder case," *The New York Times*, 8 January 1990.

"Guilt in Boston murder is lifted, but not tainted," *The New York Times*, 8 January 1990.

"Awakening after Boston nightmare," *The New York Times*, 10 January 1990.

"Police find gun linked to Boston man in killing of pregnant wife," *Chicago Tribune*, 10 January 1990.

"Gun found in river believed to be Boston murder weapon," *Chicago Sun-Times*, 10 January 1990.

"Murder hoax revives Boston's race troubles," *Chicago Sun-Times*, 11 January 1990.

"Death and deception in Boston: Anger in search of a target," *Chicago Tribune*, 11 January 1990.

"Boston murder suspect sought a brother's help, lawyer says," *The New York Times*, 12 January 1990.

"Bias and recklessness are charged in Boston reporting of Stuart slaying," *The New York Times*, 14 January 1990.

"Stuart's lie: An American tragedy," *The New York Times*, 14 January 1990.

"Murder in which motive leaves questions and chills," *The New York Times*, 15 January 1990.

"How lies can fan flames of racism," *Chicago Defender*, 16 January 1990.

"Three cases raise questions on Boston police method," *The New York Times*, 18 January 1990.

"Boston Black leaders ask for investigations," *Pittsburgh Courier*, 20 January 1990.

"Glimpses behind the hoax of Charles

Stuart," *Chicago Tribune*, 21 January 1990.

"Stuart kin offer scholarship to ease Boston race tension," *Chicago Sun-Times*, 26 January 1990.

"Minorities play second fiddle on network newscasts," *Chicago Sun-Times*, 5 February 1990.

"Pincham hints 'hypocrisy' in Phelan's quitting club," *Chicago Sun-Times*, 14 February 1990.

"Vassar students take over campus building," *Chicago Defender*, 17 February 1990."

"Aunt Jemima turns 100 years old; Continues to improve," *Chicago Defender*, 19 February 1990.

"Phelan's old club par for the course," *Chicago Tribune*, 22 February 1990.

"Uneasy pieces when collectors pursue relics from a past that can be painful to recall," *Chicago Tribune*, 25 February 1990.

"Student offended by professor's use of racial term in discussion," *Loyola Phoenix*, 23 March 1990.

"U.S. Rep. Collins launches probe of Loyola University," *Chicago Defender*, 26 March 1990.

"Slur triggers show down at Loyola," *Chicago Defender*, 29 March 1990.

"Films go 'backwards' on racism, Lee says," *Chicago Sun-Times*, 2 April 1990.

"Why Tolerate the Campus Bigots," *The New York Times*, 6 April 1990.

"Readers Can't See Themselves in the News," *USA Today*, 6 April 1990.

"Law Schools Boycotted by Minority Teachers," *The New York Times*, 6 April 1990.

"City colleges take twice as long to get degree," *Chicago Sun-Times*, 6 April 1990.

"Tennis, anyone? Country clubs may be old line, but they are a nouveau revival," *Wall Street Journal*, 12 April 1990.

"Black students can't hide from racism," *Chicago Sun-Times*, 13 April 1990.

"Loyola struggles to handle new racial tensions," *Chicago Tribune*, 15 April 1990.

"The various faces of American racism," *Chicago Defender*, 16 April 1990.

"The reluctant saviour Spike Lee lays it out: minority obstacles invite no easy answers," *Chicago Tribune*, 22 April 1990.

ADDITIONAL SOURCES

Black Economic Press, An Agenda for the '90s, Ed. by Margaret C. Sims. Joint Center for Political Studies, Washington, D.C., 1988.

Black Initiative and Government Responsibility, Introduction by John Hope Franklin and Eleanor Holmes Norton. Joint Center for Political Studies, Washington, D.C., 1987.

Black Student Council, Loyola University, Chicago, Press statement read March 22, 1990, by Council President Chenelle M. Winters.

Chicago Community Trust Human Relations Task Force Report on Race Ethics and Religious Tensions in Chicago, By the staff of the *Chicago Tribune*, September 1989.

Collins, Sharon M, *Pathway to the Top: Black Mobility in the Business World; a Doctoral Dissertation*. Northwestern University, Evanston, Ill., June 1988.

Freeman, R. "Black Economic Progress After 1964: Who Has Gained and Why," National Bureau of Economic Research, Working Paper No. 282, Cambridge, Mass., November 1978.

"Frontline: Racism 101," WGBH-TV, May 10, 1988.

"Frontline: Racism 101," WGBH-TV, February 20, 1990.

Jobs for Americans, Congressional Quarterly Inc., Washington, D.C., 1978.

Morris, Dean. *Pride Against Prejudice: Work in the Lives of Older Blacks and Young Puerto Rican Workers; The Conservation of Human Resources,* Columbia University, New York, 1969. Prepared under special grant #71-34-70-04 for the U.S. Department of Labor.

Racial Discrimination on Campus, National Association of Student Personnel Administrators, Northern Illinois University, DeKalb, Ill., 1988.

Role of the Mass Media in American Politics, Annals of the American Academy of Political and Social Science, September 1989.

Visions of a Better Way; A Black Appraisal of Public Schooling, Preface by John Hope Franklin. Joint Center for Political Studies, Washington, D.C., 1989.

Westmoreland, Sandra R., Statement, Jan. 30, 1990.

Women in Management; Career and Family Issues, Ed. by Jenny Farley, L.R. Press, Cornell University, Ithaca, N.Y., 1983.

LETTERS

Banks, Seymour, Letter to Frank Gardner, August 26, 1965.

Campbell, Ronald F., Letter to Frank Gardner, October 2, 1967.

Coyne, Mrs. John R., Letter from Illinois Sesquicentennial Commission, September 20, 1967.

Despres, Leon, Letter to Frank Gardner January 2, 1967.

Gini, Al, Letter to members of the Loyola community, March 23, 1990.

Hannon, Joseph P., Memo to Frank Gardner, April 26, 1984.

Hawkins, Barbara A., Letter to Frank Gardner, November 3, 1967.

Hodges, Roger E., Letter to Frank Gardner, June 8, 1968.

McCourt, Kathleen, Letter to Sandra R. Westmoreland, February 19, 1990.

Mikva, Mrs. Abner, Letter to the editor *Chicago Sun-Times,* February 25, 1968.

Redmond, James F., Letter to Frank Gardner, August 11, 1967.

Redmond, James F., Letter to Frank Gardner, February 14, 1968.

Smith, Edith F., Letter to Frank Gardner, January 17, 1968.

Solomon, Jean M., Letter to Frank Gardner, July 11, 1968.

INDEX

A

"A Different World," 22
Aaron, Hank, 15
Abbott Hall, Northwestern University (Chicago, Ill.), 16
Aberdeen Proving Ground, 115
Abolition of fraternities and sororities, 181
Abrams, Robert, 100, 101
Academy Awards, 78
Accra, Ghana, 183
Affirmative action, 58, 130
African American Real Estate Man, viii
Alabama A&M College (Normal, Ala.), 6
Alabama State College, 6
Alpha Kappa Alpha Sorority, 118
American Bar Association, 18
American Broadcasting Co. (ABC), 79, 80
American Institute of Banking, 104
American Legion Post, 154
Amherst, Ma., 175
"An Autobiography of Black Chicago," vii
"An Autobiography of Black Jazz," vii
"An Autobiography of Black Politics," vii
Ann Arbor, Mich., 179
Anti-racist activity, viii
Arlen, Harold, 102
Armstrong, Louis, 44, 115
Asians, 120, 121
Athens, Ga., 148, 180
Atlanta, Ga., 108, 119, 180
Atlanta public schools, 180
Atlanta University (Atlanta, Ga.), 6

Lunceford, Jimmy, 115

M

Madden, Owney, 115
Madison, Franklin, 23–33
Madison, Wisc., 180
Madrid, Spain, 150
Magnet schools, 141
Main Bank (Chicago, Ill.), 106
Main post office (Chicago, Ill.), 133
Malcolm X, 63
Manhattan, NY, 114
Manley, Aubry, 166
Man-made barriers, 171
Marshall, Thurgood, 21
Marshall Field's Department Store (Chicago, Ill.), 21
Marx, Miriam, 101
Massachusetts Institute of Technology, MIT (Cambridge, Mass.), 50, 86, 87
Matney, Bill, 79
Mayflower Hotel (Chicago, Ill.), 108, 109
Maynard, Robert, 84
Mays, Joshua, 85
Mays, Mary Belle, 85
Mays, Willard, 85–101
Maywood, Ill., 102
McBride, Fran, 178
McConner, Ora, 145
McCormick, Robert R., 79
McCosh Elementary School, 161
McCourt, Kathleen, 177
McHugh, Jimmy, 102
"Me and My Shadow," 45
Medical Associates (Chicago, Ill.), 165–167
Melnick, Chris, 136, 137
Mercy Hospital (Chicago, Ill.), 166
Merriweather, Harry, 45, 46
Michael Reese Hospital (Chicago, Ill.), 165, 167
Michigan Chronicle (Detroit, Mich.), 79